OUR TREES OF LIFE

OUR TREES OF LIFE

The Darkening Sky Over Christ's Believers

CHRISTINE GRAEF

Introduction by Thomas Miess-McDonald

RESOURCE *Publications* · Eugene, Oregon

OUR TREES OF LIFE
The Darkening Sky Over Christ's Believers

Copyright © 2015 Christine Graef. All rights reserved. Except for brief quotations in critical publications or reviews, no part of this book may be reproduced in any manner without prior written permission from the publisher. Write: Permissions, Wipf and Stock Publishers, 199 W. 8th Ave., Suite 3, Eugene, OR 97401.

Resource Publication
An Imprint of Wipf and Stock Publishers
199 W. 8th Ave., Suite 3
Eugene, OR 97401

www.wipfandstock.com

ISBN 13: 978-1-4982-3153-4

Manufactured in the U.S.A. 10/26/2015

Scripture quotation marked (NIV) are taken from the Holy Bible, New International Version, NIV, Copyright 1973, 1978, 1984, 2011 by Biblica Inc. Used by permission of Zondervan. All rights reserved worldwide. www.zondervan.com The "NIV" and "New International Version"are trademarks registered in the United States Patent and Trademark Office by Biblica, Inc.

Blessed are those who wash their robes, that they may have the right to the tree of life and may go through the gates into the city. (Rev 22:14)

CONTENTS

Introduction by Thomas Miess-McDonald | ix

1   NORTH AMERICA | 1
2   SOUTH AMERICA | 21
3   EUROPE | 40
4   AFRICA | 58
5   ASIA | 75
6   AUSTRALIA | 94
7   ANTARCTICA | 112

Bibliography | 131

INTRODUCTION

The great tree soared heavenward, its long roots stretching out to the North, South, East, and West. A magnificent bird perched upon the crown of the tree, nothing escaped its ever-watchful eyes. The tree was the Tree of Peace, its roots which are known as the White Roots of Peace would carry the message of the Creator's Peace to the four directions, the weapons of war were buried under its roots, and an Eagle perched upon the top of the Peace Tree to warn the people of anything that would come to disturb their peace.

This great tree is the White Pine, the largest, tallest tree on the east of North America. Long ago, before the arrival of the Europeans the Creator sent a man known as the Peacemaker to teach the way of peace to the Iroquoian peoples.

Peacemaker chose the White Pine because it holds its needles in bunches of five. The bunch of five needles would represent the original five nations of the Iroquoian Confederacy, the Mohawk, Oneida, Seneca, Onondaga, and Cayuga who form the Confederacy of peace. The Tree of Peace is still the symbol of the Iroquoian Confederacy. Its teaching is useful and valuable to us today.

In a time even much longer ago then the founding of the Iroquoian Confederacy, we see the mention of the Creator's interaction with humankind through the use of trees:

"And the Lord God made all kinds of trees grow out of the ground- trees that were pleasing to the eye and good for food. In the middle of the garden were the tree of life and the tree of the knowledge of good and evil."(Gen 2:9)

In the Garden of Eden, humankind received the mandate to work together with the Creator, to be good and responsible stewards and servants of the Creation. We are called to be protectors, not destroyers of the Creation.

This mandate still stands today but, as we look around our world, we see the words and teaching of our Creator sadly ignored, disbelieved or distorted. Man has not been a good and responsible caretaker of God's Creation. Humankind has spent most of its time creating weapons of war rather than living peaceably as our Father intended us to live.

The Creation including humankind and the trees, which God has used consistently on every continent to speak to us, is in trouble. Overt consumerism and a lack of awareness of the results of actions, have set the Creation on course with disaster of an unprecedented scale.

How profound and wise is the teaching that speaks of those who follow the way of the Creator:

"That person is like a tree planted by streams of water, which yields its fruit in season and whose leaf does not wither . . . Whatever they do prospers." (Ps 1:3)

In the Jewish Mishnah we see reference to To B' Shevat which is the new year for trees. During this time appropriate foods are eaten which are abundant in Israel and trees are planted. Another purpose of the Tu B'Shevat is to calculate the age of trees for tithing. This is first mentioned in Lev 19:23–25.

Our Creator has inexorably linked our lives with that of the trees. Trees have served as instruction and teaching directly from our Creator. Trees are an indicator of the health of the Creation. Trees are the lungs of the planet and serve countless other functions.

In this book, Christine Graef takes us on a Journey to all seven continents. It is a trek with our Creator and his creation, the trees.

Introduction

    This is a Journey that is very close to my heart since my Native name is Karontes which means long (big) tree. The implication of my name is that I would be like a big tree and many people would take shelter under my branches. I have always had a special bond with and love for trees and as a child I spent much of my day in the woods, alone among the trees with God's creation. Even today, I find that I must be surrounded by trees. Trees speak the language of our Creator. God is revealed to us through the stillness and quiet of the forest.

    As I read this book, I find it to be a blessing to my spirit, There is much wisdom to be found within these pages which provide the reader with a very unique intertwining of Natural History, Ecology and Theology. A rare blend indeed.

Rev. Thomas Miess-McDonald,
Bear Clan, Metis Nation, Th.D.

1

NORTH AMERICA

He cut down cedars, or perhaps took a cypress or oak. He let it grow among the trees of the forest, or planted a pine, and the rain made it grow. (Isa 44:14)

High winds blast through pillars of clouds blowing so strong that stellar jets leave trails of cold dust through miles of space. Debris is flung around burning balls of light at supersonic speeds as they collapse into dense globes. Lightning flashes as a 60 mph storm fires up the sky. Forty thousand mile magnetic pulls whip funnels of hot gas into tornadoes that span the size of earth. Spinning at speeds of more than a million miles per hour it sparks electrical currents into the ionosphere powering auroras like the northern lights. Somewhere in the constellation Aquarius comets that would have orbited a star are suddenly tossed into each other, kicking up celestial dust storms as collisions and mergers build a kingdom of galaxies. Fueled by heat, fashioned by friction, asteroids as large as mountains speed by on their way into deep space. Swirling around Saturn celestial gases crash, massive clouds of hydrogen mixing with oxygen, sulfur, and other elements sculpt orange-red glows that separate into green streams of light.

Luminous blue stars, white stars, violet, red, and orange shine through the heavens. Earth hurtles through the stars at eighteen miles per second, smashing through stone fragments, storms of meteor fireballs showering the heavens, and comets with million mile tails, held in the gravity of a star 93 million miles away.

An ordinary star turning counterclockwise, the sun's rays stream 186,000 miles per second at the speed of light, churning up solar flares shooting millions of tons of charged particles toward earth as it pulls the planets around a wheel. Earth is electrified with some 40,000 thunderstorms every day, more than a thousand storms of lightning every moment. The moon pulls bulges of ocean water on the side of the planet rotating closest to its light. The crust covering earth releases seismic waves millions of times every year. The tremors quake across the land, shifting earth to landslides, sending up a force from the ocean bottom into tsunamis. Volcanoes awaken. The trade winds, the westerlies, and polar winds ceaselessly work to redistribute heat in the atmosphere as the earth spins round and round.

We are born into the middle of raging storms.

God has not left us without shelter. Like a bird safely nested in the arms of a tree when the storm winds blow all around her, we've been given a promise passed to us through generations of believers willing to suffer and die so the truth could be heard.

She is a tree of life to those who take hold of her; those who hold her fast will be blessed (Prov 3:18).

God created earth to bloom an array of trees in the world he knew his son would come to save. The trees became the pictorial language ancient in its tradition of shelter, spiritual growth, transformation, and markers of consecrated places and times across all lands. Trees are seen as archetypes of consciousness and of creation, gates to heaven and roots to the past. Found in the Shamanic, Hindu, Egyptian, Sumerian, Toltec, Mayan, Native, Norse, Celtic, Judaic, and Christian traditions, trees are a universal language understood on each of earth's seven continents.

North America

North America is the third largest of the continents at 9.54 million square miles. One of the last continents free to worship Jesus, it covers about 17 percent of the earth's land and is home to about 8 percent of the people, 529 million who are both the original people of the land and the Europeans and others who have migrated here.

Nearly all the old growth forests in the east were cleared for agriculture, urban development, or left for second growth forests now devoid of American chestnuts and under attack by invasive species colonizing the land. The vast lands of oak in the Midwest were cleared for corn fields. In the Northwest ancient forests were cut down to be planted with monocultures of one type of tree in checkerboard patterns. More than 256 miles of forest were cleared to make way for mining oil sands near the Athabasca River in Alberta. In the southern continent the small yew tree only grows on bluffs and ravines along the Apalachicola River. Adult trees have been dying and young seedlings replacing them are few. Science has not yet figured out why. The tree's bark contains taxol, discovered in 1971 to treat cancer. Critically endangered, it is not yet known what future medicine may yet be discovered in its roots, trunk, branches, seeds, or foliage.

Transformed under sun's light dappling the floors where the seeds wait, a tree sends signals to its roots to begin new growth in the moist soil. Aspens reach for full sun next to black cherry, oak, and birch. Deer browse among the young trees. Beavers come and create wetlands. Woodpeckers and owls find food and shelter in the older trees. Ruffed grouse come for the mature flower buds. The aspen ages and thins, and the pines, oaks, and maples grow tall as the sunlight reaches them.

Under winter's low gray sky, exhausted from their fruitfulness, the trees drop their precious jewels. Empty nests rest on bare silent branches, but the leaves did not fall without presenting their promise. Nothing has been lost. Trees hold their new flowers and leaves wrapped in buds biding their time for the warm light of spring to signal them to unfurl, come and grow toward the light. Having developed in the summer months, the hickories hold clusters of tiny leaves. The beginning of a flower is in the birch, alder, and hazelnuts. Larger buds are on the ash and the poplars. Through the cold months deer, mice and rabbits nibble on the buds, twigs and roots, the promise of the spring sustaining them. Finches are kept by maple flower buds. Squirrels find nourishment in the tips of balsam firs.

The eastern white pine stands among its companions of oaks, hickories, elms, beeches, and poplars supporting more than 200 species of butterflies and moths and charms of black-capped chickadees. The flames of autumn in earth's temperate zones consume every green leaf except the tribes of evergreens that remain witness to the far off heaven still present in the benediction of the morning. White-tailed deer and cottontails, beaver and mourning doves depend on the evergreen's bark to help them through winter months. Its niches house woodpeckers and squirrels. Bald eagles favor them for nest sites high above the ground and its dense green foliage protects from winds and cold. The pine can live more than four centuries, feeding chipmunks and meadow voles with its pine needles and seeds and keeping its green leaves when the frost comes and then the snow. Warblers and nuthatches too depend on the seeds inside the pinecones maturing from small yellow cone flowers.

Winter brings birds and animals in search of branches of shelter or to lay dormant snuggled safely by its roots. Yet not all the animals and not every bird will survive to see God make a new day. Some will pass away never knowing the warmth again as birds return with their songs and squirrels chase each other beneath the sun. The trees green and deer are born to a new season without them.

Not everyone will know there is a bright morning star that will dawn after frost blankets the valley a sun of righteousness with healing in its light moving across the earth. A soul may wither not hearing of the tree of life calming the storm or the words softening the hardened soil with dew, resting like God's spirit on a soul. They will not stand among the fresh flowering grasses and new growth if the words of life are silenced.

North America

Unleashed across the ocean to the shores of North America, Christianity became a standard of neighborhood morality and the identity of government. The Bible arrived with reverence for its place in the home and community.

You, my brothers and sisters, were called to be free. But do not use your freedom to indulge the flesh; rather, serve one another humbly in love (Gal 5:13).

But after five centuries of congregating on the continent with liberty to live under God's laws, the Bible is obscured and faded into the background as light vanishes in the dusk. Canada's national motto, "From Sea to Sea," was adopted in 1921, derived from Psalm 72:8, "May he rule from sea to sea and from the river to the ends of the earth." In 1956 "In God We Trust" became America's motto. By the 1990s a rise in spiritual quests sought grafting in every idea outside of God's water of life. A decade later the name of Jesus was being banned as an extremist, offensive movement.

North America is wandering away from its nest in the tree of life. In place of the consensus of Bible basics, rationalizations woven from the twigs of the tree of knowledge question the authority of God. Jesus is not saying what we want him to say or being the worldly king that his crucifiers had expected of him to elevate us with wealth and power. Policies are emptying the land of Jesus.

A great light dawned when Jesus came to his people. Let there be light, God said as he began the creation. He sent light again to create a new man from fallen humanity. This light is the glory of God, and the Lamb is the light. (Rev 21:23).

After Jesus declared his faith when he was baptized in the Jordan, the tempter came to Jesus asking him to turn stones into bread, to test God to keep him safe even if he threw himself off the highest point of the temple, or to rule the world's kingdoms (Matt 4:1–11) Jesus was uncompromising.

Man shall not live on bread alone, but on every word that comes from the mouth of God.

It is also written: Do not put the Lord your God to the test.

Worship the Lord your God, and serve him only.

Inclined to choose the tree of knowledge to feed our hunger, fulfill our earthly wishes for our own desires and ignore the words of the crucifixion, the very temptations we ask of God when we compromise his teachings are the issues Jesus refused. Accepting every word of his Father and believing the consequences for our lives if we don't, Jesus held the narrow path we are intended to travel. Rooted in God's will, he comes bringing the source of living water to graft others into the branches.

As the heart of North America struggles for its soul, blizzards strike the northeast, tornadoes rip through the nation, rivers flow over their shores in deluges never before this frequent, drought brings wildfires to scorch thousands of acres. The continent moves into the edge of the storm against Jesus. The words of Christ are being hunted down, stalked like the deer in Psalm 42 left panting for water, weakened and desperate, running for its life when the shelter of the tree is gone.

On December 19, 2014 a teacher at Helen Hunt-Jackson Elementary School in Temecula, California gave her first grade students the assignment to bring something from home that represented a family Christmas tradition.[1] Fox News reported that six-year-old Brynn Williams brought the Star of Bethlehem from the top of the Christmas tree to represent why her family celebrated Christmas. "The three kings followed the star to find baby Jesus, the savior of the world," she told the classroom. Before she could recite John 3:16, "For God so loved the world that he gave his one and only Son, that whoever believes in him shall not perish but have eternal life," the teacher ordered Brynn to "Stop right there," and Brynn was told to take her seat. The school explained that Brynn was not allowed to speak about the Bible in school to protect others from being offended.

God continues to say, Let there be light.

The first blessing Jesus speaks in the book of Revelation tells of the importance of speaking the message out loud. "Blessed is the one who reads aloud the words of this prophecy" (Rev 1:3). Yet

---

1. Fox News, "CA Teacher Tells 1st-Grader to Stop Talking About the Bible"

the branches Jesus has grafted to bring the words of faith are being broken off and tossed on the ground. We go to the water but it's become polluted and causes illness instead of refreshing. We sit in the sun's warmth but are told the sky will cause skin cancers. We want to teach our children about the beauty God designed for man and woman in marriage but we are taken into court for speaking in the name of Jesus. Our children grow with trust in their hearts needing their fathers to give their hand into a protective marriage, but they are cast down with disconnect by society's immoral messages and left in pervasive depression, a life betrayed. "Hope deferred makes the heart sick, but a longing fulfilled is a tree of life" (Prov 13:12).

The continent suffers in its soil, its water, its air. The minds of the people are clouded by doctrines of self-appeasement. But light, the signature of God, can never be polluted. God's instructions pouring in waves and particles on every nation are unchangeable, undeniable.

Jesus let us know, "There is a judge for the one who rejects me and does not accept my words; the very words I have spoken will condemn them at the last day" (John 12:48), because he did not speak his own message but the message of God flashing from heaven on rays of light, breaking the darkness, illuminating all that is around us, stirring the seeds to send out tap roots, bringing forth new leaves emerging to capture the grace of his light.

We know the promised birth of spring is arriving because more light is over us. The season returns with winds from the south encountering winds sent from the east, rains, and cold fronts from the west encouraging the trees to put on their garments of praise. Orioles and tanagers by the dozens, warblers, and buntings all return to the trees. Skeins of geese honk across the sky northward. Soaring ospreys and hawks take routes along the mountains to glide on updrafts created from heat on earth's surface. Sugar maple seeds germinate soon after snow melts, yellow birch beside it waits longer for temperatures to warm. A descent of woodpeckers gather to tend God's ash trees after the emerald ash borer decimated millions of trees. The larvae bores through the bark, disrupting the flow of water and nutrients. The woodpecker won't save the tree after it's been harmed, but it will save the forest by foraging the bark to reduce the beetle's spread to other trees. Deciduous forests are shifting northward with warming temperatures. Their berries, seeds, and bugs are moving with them bringing whole populations of birds and animals to follow. Trees stand against borers chewing through the wood, beetles eating young shoots, and miners eating their leaves. Jack pine budworm, bark beetles, gypsy moths, sawflies, white pine tip weevil, sugar maple borer, and aphids all prey on the health of North America.

The trees mediate for the earth as nature recovers the fallen leaves to bring new growth. The leaves purify the air to give earth one breath shared by all. They circulate the water to give rivers, lakes, and the return of rainfall.

The ministry of the leaves heals all nations.

These giants of the land struggle against their foes, the worms, frost, hail, parched lands, and toxic air. More than 40,000 invasive species coming in with trade from Europe and Asia such as purple loosestrife are overtaking wetlands.[2] Buckthorn is disrupting ecological cycles of food chains and threatening the survival of already endangered species by preventing native species from re-growing. The prophet Isaiah said the trees would also be misused for carving idols "and the things they treasure are worthless" (Isa 44:9).

You will be like an oak with fading leaves, like a garden without water (Isa 1:30).

God spoke about the renewing cycles in nature showing us our need to revive our minds and bodies to cleanse continually from the world's dust and to remain rooted in his Spirit. He has promised to supply all our needs for our growth.

Sometimes that need is for the storm. The solemn dark winds that beat down the leaves refine a community, pushing roots deeper to acquire more strength. The clouds are blown away, leaves sparkle seeing the sun has always been there, dripping raindrops from the arms of trees, sprayed with light as the sun washes over,

---

2. Cook, "Some Exotic Species Are Useful and Benign"

glistening and transforming the heart of all it touches as it brings alive new creations.

"My father is the gardener," Jesus said. "He cuts off every branch in me that bears no fruit, while every branch that does bear fruit he prunes so that it will be even more fruitful" (John 15:1–2). It's to God's glory that we bear fruit that shows we are the disciples of Jesus (v7). "If you keep my commands, you will remain in my love, just as I have kept my Father's commands and remain in his love." The pruning may come in a flood that strips away our surroundings, but it will bring about joy "so that your joy may be complete" (v11).

No branch can bear fruit by itself, he said. It must remain in the vine.

The world goes on as if Jesus rising to the throne made no difference. Words falling like leaves from the trees are being swept up by a whirlwind of arguments bringing about talk of God, to question, listen, and choose between the tree of life and the tree of knowledge that is always in the gardens of earth, tempting us to use our own knowledge for ways to take care of ourselves. Lost fellowship with God leaves us without water, no longer rooted in the source that flows through us when we are rooted in God's will. We become prone to the voices leading us elsewhere and subdue our minds to fit in with political correctness and avoid the sneers of others. The hoped for results searched for in the tree of knowledge have left the world thirsting for life. Yet Christ who quenched thirst offended everyone, especially religious leaders, to the point they killed him.

Blessed is the one who perseveres under trial because, having stood the test, that person will receive the crown of life that the Lord has promised to those who love him (James 1:12).

God's women, his men, and his children are being stalked by a power wanting to control. Missionaries to a fallen culture, they are now ridiculed and banished from policies, education, military, and families. Symbols of worship are destroyed as churches and Bibles are burned and scriptures are removed from public places. Control is taken as the judiciary bans the use of the name of Jesus.

A predator brings intimidation, intends fear, causing the victim to move away from where they stand or shrink from growth in the full sunlight. Jesus was stalked throughout his life from the time he was born to the time he was taken to the cross. The apostle Paul was stalking Christians before he transformed, then he was stalked and had to be let out in a basket through a window to escape his predators. Peter was targeted too in Acts 12:1–3. "It was about this time that King Herod arrested some who belonged to the church, intending to persecute them. He had James, the brother of John, put to death with the sword. When he saw that this met with approval among the Jews, he proceeded to seize Peter also." John the Baptist was stalked, imprisoned, and beheaded. In the end of days the Antichrist will stalk all those who don't worship him and silence them with death.

At times the prey feels so trapped and helpless that they wish to die. Jezebel and Ahab called Elijah a troublemaker and blamed him for the drought. Elijah responds by telling them it is they who troubled the land by not serving the living God. Bold in his relationship with God, Elijah takes twelve stones, pours saturating amounts of water on an altar and speaks simply asking God to light it so the people will know the Lord God. Immediately the soaking wet alter is ignited from heaven. Jezebel's false prophets are seized and put to death.

Despite this proclamation of God's presence, when Jezebel threatens to take his life Elijah runs a day's journey away to sit beneath a tree. So overwhelmed by threats he prayed that he'd die. "I have had enough, LORD," he said. (1Kgs 19:4) Emptied, he fell asleep.

As he slept an angel touched him, calling his name to tell Elijah that God understands his needed rest. The journey is too much even for this man of faith. The angel gave him warm baked bread and fresh water to strengthen him and left him beneath the tree to rest deeply.

Strengthened, Elijah traveled forty days and forty nights to reach Horeb, the mountain of God, where he retreated into a cave. He heard the wind that brings a destroying storm. He saw the fire which brings judgment. Then the still small voice of God stirred him back to action. Those entrusted with the concern of Jesus are given a glimpse of the splendor, the glorious brightness of his kingdom unveiled to strengthen their roots in the living waters. Sixty years after he had known Jesus on earth, John saw Jesus ascended in his glory. John had been banished to the rocky island of Patmos in the Aegean Sea, a small place of about thirteen square miles. At a time when the earth was filled with about 100 million people and the loss of forest was leading to the collapse the Roman Empire, John sees Christ in the midst of lamp stands that signify the church.

He stands at the very center of the church, shining waves of light, illuminating a spectrum of colors. Jesus is still among us, knowing our part in this story and the attempts to take our sight away from him. He will sustain those who stand like trees of conscience speaking the uncompromising words that are leaves greening a tree and supporting the need for light.

Who is my neighbor, an expert in law asked Jesus. Jesus replied, the one who brings mercy does the will of God. Mercy to Jesus meant bringing a person back to relationship with God. It intends words teaching about spiritual warfare that cannot be perpetuated through compromise. We learn of the promise because of those who spoke what Jesus wanted us to know, "Now when these things begin to happen, look up and lift up your heads, because your redemption draws near" (Luke 21:2)

The small cloud once on the distant horizon of North America is now overhead, casting its shadow, stretching its ranks like a curtain across the sun. Like the days of Noah, a flood is ripping through the land, uprooting the trees, knocking down the imploring voice of God. North America is caught unaware of the gathering storm darkening the sky as those who enter the safety of the ark of salvation set the alarm to warn of intrusion of the stalker. Using a language no human hears, the willows, poplars, and sugar maples warn each other about insect attacks. The trees nearby hear what their neighbors are experiencing through a chemical reaction emitted by the wounded tree. The other trees begin releasing

Our Trees of Life

volatiles to defend themselves. The trees form a network of signals to preserve their community's foliage.

I have not run away from being your shepherd (Jer 17:16).

In March 2014 Fox News reported that an Air Force Academy cadet was ordered to remove a passage from scripture he'd written on his white board outside his dorm room because it offended non-Christians and could cause "subordinates to doubt the leader's religious impartiality."[3] The passage read, "I have been crucified with Christ therefore I no longer live, but Christ lives in me" (Gal 2:20). Twenty-nine cadets and four faculty and staff reportedly complained about the verse.

In Georgia, high school students at Augusta's Alleluia Community School were forbidden to sing traditional holiday songs that celebrate the birth of Christ to veterans at the Veterans Affairs hospital in December 2013.[4] In Texas children at Grace Academy in Prosper spent the last Friday before school vacation making Christmas cards for bedridden veterans at the VA hospital in Dallas. In thought that the veterans may have no family nearby or not know anyone there, the children wanted them to know they were not forgotten. But the veterans never saw the cards because Christmas cards violate VA policy.[5]

In the face of strengthening head winds we are told believers will prevail.

They will be like a tree planted by the water that sends out its roots by the stream. It does not fear when heat comes; its leaves are always green. It has no worries in a year of drought and never fails to bear fruit (Jer 17:8).

The fruit of the Spirit is love, joy, peace, forbearance, kindness, goodness, faithfulness, gentleness and self-control (Gal 5:22–23).

The description begins with love. Jesus said, "As I have loved you, so you must love one another" (John 13:34). He sets priority

---

3. Todd, "What's-going-on-at-Air-Force-Academy-God's-Word-vs-Pentagon's-Word"

4. CBS News, "Hospital Bans Christmas Carolers From Singing Religious Song"

5. Sedlock, "Mish"

on relationship. The fruit of love is a thirst for others the way Christ thirsted for us to be saved from the destroyer and restored to relationship with his Father. A distinguishing trait of God is how he grows through us when we're rooted in his water of life. Paul says no matter what other gifts we have, we are nothing if we don't have this love that desires the redemption of another.

> Love is patient, love is kind. It does not envy, it does not boast, it is not proud. It does not dishonor others, it is not self-seeking, it is not easily angered, it keeps no record of wrongs. Love does not delight in evil but rejoices with the truth. It always protects, always trusts, always hopes, always perseveres.

Love never fails (1Cor:4–8).

Greater love has no one than this: to lay down one's life for one's friends (John 15:13).

The leaf in spring testifies to its need for the faded leaves on the ground. Delicate and fragile, in every size, form, color, and texture, the leaf is the strength of the tree, the leaf is the servant, laboring for the entire tree to grow tall and strong, standing watch through the days of warm sun, nights of starlight peeking through its branches. On the threshold of autumn the days draw in. The woodland becomes somber as we prepare for the frost that will fade the leaf's colors. Still facing the sun, knowing God knows every sparrow and every leaf that falls, leaves drop from their stems to flutter, heaping them on the ground. Still they continue to labor by becoming nutrients for the deep roots that sustain next year's leaves.

At great risk to their lives, jobs, and friendships, those chosen to believe Jesus ache for the lost and broken to listen. Standing up, Paul motioned with his hand and said: "Fellow Israelites and you Gentiles who worship God, listen to me! (Acts 13:16)

This is my Son, whom I love; with him I am well pleased. Listen to him! (Matt 17:3–5)

Whoever listens to you listens to me; whoever rejects you rejects me; but whoever rejects me rejects him who sent me (Luke 10:16).

She had a sister called Mary, who sat at the Lord's feet listening to what he said (Luke 10:39).

One of those listening was a woman from the city of Thyatira named Lydia, a dealer in purple cloth. She was a worshiper of God. The Lord opened her heart to respond to Paul's message (Acts 16:14).

In 2013 Canada's Supreme Court voted to repress Christians who speak against sin as defined by the Bible.[6] The February 27 decision in Saskatchewan, Human Rights Commission v. Whatcott, found Christian pro-family activist William Whatcott guilty of hate speech for distributing flyers to neighborhoods in Saskatoon and Regina that spoke against homosexual practices. Finding no discernment between Christianity's principles that we are to hate the sin while having brotherly love to save the sinner, the court ordered William to pay the legal fees of the Human Rights Commission, $7,500 to the two homosexuals offended by the flyers, and designated a fine for anyone who promotes religious teachings interpreted as hate speech.

Pursued, slandered, reviled, the ones whose voices transcend like trees rising on the skyline to absorb light from the mercy throne for the hurting world are considered blessed by God because God can abide with them.

They will be called oaks of righteousness, a planting of the Lord for the display of his splendor (Isa 61:3). God will bestow on them a crown of beauty. To replace the mourning, God will clothe them in a garment of praise.

Life with God will demand a response to Jesus from every person as North America transforms into policy and education that prohibit his instructions. What will happen to those left perishing if we do not tell them with words God intended.

Consequently, faith comes from hearing the message, and the message is heard through the word about Christ (Rom 10:17).

In May 2014 Worthy News reported Liberty Counsel, a Christian legal group defending a pastor who was arrested for protesting outside an abortion clinic in Mississippi. Pastor Stephen

---

6. Culture News, "Supremes Rule Bible as Hate Speech in Canada"

Joiner was jailed for carrying a sign saying that abortion kills children, charged with obstructing a local parade ordinance although he was alone.[7] Worthy News reported in June 2014 that for the first time in forty years evangelicals at Bowdoin College will not be allowed to meet as a student club to study the Bible, pray, and worship. The Bowdoin Christian Fellowship is no longer recognized on campus by a college caught in the dispute between religious freedoms and government anti-discrimination policies. The axe is falling in every segment of society. A hospital employee was ordered to remove "God Bless America" from her email signature.[8] In Phoenix, Arizona Pastor Michael Salman served a sixty-day sentence in Maricopa County for holding a home Bible study that allegedly violated city building codes.[9]

> Also I gave them my Sabbaths as a sign between us, so they would know that I the Lord made them holy (Ezek 20:12). There remains, then, a Sabbath-rest for the people of God; for anyone who enters God's rest also rests from their works, just as God did from his. Let us, therefore, make every effort to enter that rest, so that no one will perish by following their example of disobedience (Heb 4:9–11).Then God blessed the seventh day and made it holy, because on it he rested from all the work of creating that he had done (Gen 2:3). Jesus said, The Sabbath was made for man, not man for the Sabbath (Mark 2:27). Remember the Sabbath day by keeping it holy (Exod 20:8).

God asked that the people turn their face toward him. He asked that the people pray. Speaking through Isaiah, God told his people:

> If you keep your feet from breaking the Sabbath and from doing as you please on my holy day, if you call the Sabbath a delight and the Lord's holy day honorable, and

---

7. DeCaro, "Pastor Jailed for Displaying Anti-Abortion Sign"

8. Worthy Christian News, "Hospital Employee Ordered to Remove God Bless America From Email Signature"

9. Vazquez, "Arizona Man Sent to Jail for Holding Bible Studies in His Home"

if you honor it by not going your own way and not doing as you please or speaking idle words, then you will find your joy in the Lord, and I will cause you to ride in triumph on the heights of the land and to feast on the inheritance of your father Jacob (Isa 58:13–14).

These are a shadow of the things that were to come; the reality, however, is found in Christ (Col 2:17).

Unique to the people of Christ is their overflowing worship of God that comes up from their roots in living water. No other organization of man provides this. When Jesus spoke of worship to the Hebrew people, they knew the word to mean *shahhah*, which means to bow down, on one's knees before God who is worthy of this respect. Paul's letter to Timothy reminded that those called by Christ are to bring a purifying effect to a world infected by selfish gains, celebrating forces that break apart families and promote gender confusion, fear, and uncertainties. He described this worship as quenching the power of fire, escaping the edge of the sword, weakness being made strong, becoming mighty in war, putting foreign armies to flight.

The sacred traditions sanctified by prayer are not keeping pace with the wave of policies overtaking the land. The 2015 Pew survey, called America's Changing Religious Landscape, showed a decline from 78.4 percent of believers in 2007 to 70.6 percent in 2015 who say they are affiliated with Christian faith.[10] The tradition of a Sunday shared through generations of families is disappearing. With each passing year church attendance does not grow along with population growth in any state or province. Among reasons cited is the blurring of the line as churches bend to the systems of society trying to make everyone feel accepted. For the spiritually mature whose needs are for the Father of light who has no shadow or turning, there's little choice but to leave.

So, because you are lukewarm—neither hot nor cold—I am about to spit you out of my mouth. I know your deeds, that you are neither cold nor hot. I wish you were either one or the other! (Rev 3:15–16).

---

10. Pew Forum, "America's Changing Religious Landscape"

North America

When temperature drops and we settle in for winter, water outside a tree's cells freezes first, a process that releases heat energy to help keep fluids inside the tree from freezing. Temperatures in the branches rise as the tree captures less solar energy to transfer into food chains. When winter closes in around the words of Jesus with mockery and disdain, we pull in and are to create heat with more prayer to preserve the life-giving waters we've been given. If my people will seek my face, God says. The responsibility to declare the praises of being called into his light (1Pet2:9) is placed on those who are called by God's name. Wake up, he echoes through the clouds and passing storms, and Christ will shine on you (Eph5:14).

Of the more than 331,000 churches of every denomination in America, only 10 percent of churches report more than 350 members, reported by the Barna Group.[11] Most Americans who attend go to the large churches where people gather yet visitors feel depersonalized and lonely. Individuals who never find a purpose in these groups fade away feeling unnoticed. As families relocate to follow employment, a sense of community is lost and serving a community through its spiritual needs never takes root.

Increasing pressure to marginalize the Bible and use law to direct its application portrays Christians as oppressors criticized for not supporting the social agenda. Evangelism is noted as a dangerous organization by the Islam State. Yet hearing the word is what leads to God. God regenerates through his words about being forgiven and how to be cleansed.

In the way the serpent tempted Eve to become a god herself, and Christ himself was offered the choice to be his own power without God, the messages being sent across North America are leading the coming generations. The Lord's Prayer asks that we not be led into temptation. We are to continually pray to avoid this.

I want to know Christ—yes, to know the power of his resurrection and participation in his sufferings, becoming like him in his death (Phil 3:10).

From God's perspective, the persecuted in Christ are like the oaks, the pines, all the branches grafted into his son promised

---

11. McGraw, "Is Christianity in America losing ground?"

the water of life, never to thirst again. The analogy lends itself to ongoing relationship with his Spirit, actively sending out roots searching for his water, trusting that it is always nearby. The tree is a continuous poem sung between the water and the root, the branches reaching to touch the hem of his garment, appearing to sleep in winter only to resurrect at the return of light.

We are washed in the word. We stand on it in Revelation's description of the sea of glass. Water is found in the soil, in the tree's internal reservoirs and below the blanket of snow insulating the ground and preventing deep freezes. When temperatures rise above freezing, the water in the sapwood and branches flows through the xylem, tubes that permit continuous columns of water to move throughout the tree. Hardwood trees renew xylem cells every spring to re-establish the water transport system. To remain green through winter conifers have valves that seal the ends of the tracheid tube many times during the season. Conifers can also diffuse water from cell to cell to meet the water demands of each part of its members when the seasons bring growth to a standstill.

Like the tree, we are to be, "rooted and built up in him, strengthened in the faith as you were taught, and overflowing with thankfulness" (Col 2:7) to continue giving and receiving the sustaining water through all seasons as the stages of fruit mature. Within the seeds passed along are the warnings of Jesus to prepare for increasing persecution.

In fact, when we were with you, we kept telling you that we would be persecuted. And it turned out that way, as you well know (1 Thess 3:4).

In fact, everyone who wants to live a godly life in Christ Jesus will be persecuted (2 Tim 3:12).

The birds and little squirrels insure that some seeds fall around the ground so that God's plan to continue his trees is fulfilled. We don't yet see in an acorn the oak tree offering haven, but growth is happening to prepare it. The winds rock it in the boughs. The birds sing to it all summer. The autumn brings it to the soil, an embryo waits inside the seed as leaves fall and cover it.

Two winters may pass over as its tiny leaves wait to unfold. The sun's warmth splits the shell and earth pulls the taproot deep in the soil where it finds water to sustain the emerging leaves. The sun welcomes the leaf unfolding helping it create chlorophyll to manufacture its food from the water in the soil and carbon dioxide in the air.

Tucked at the base of the leaves is a bud that is dividing cells to grow upward into a tall tree stretching toward the sky. Flowers grow around it. Butterflies come and the rabbits, chipmunks, deer, and birds who depend on it come. People come and draw strength from finding the roots of the elders sustained by God's words in the past.

Like sparrows we pick up twigs from all of these trees and bring them to our nests.

Woden, a mythological English figure, is said to have tied himself on the ash tree and fasted for nine days and nights to gain access to life's mysteries. The tree was considered a doorway connecting the spiritual world with the physical. Places the oak, ash, and hawthorn grow together are said to be special, a place that allows imagination for fairies to work wishes. The European ash tree is called Yugdrasill, the World Tree that originated other life, its early spring flowers pollinating before the tree leafed. The Branching Tree of Uisneach planted by Fintan the Ancient was an ash marking the center of Ireland. In North America its logs are pounded to peel strips of splints along the grain for baskets. Birch tree bark is also used to create baskets for food and storage. Now on the threatened list, birch shares with the ash its use as a symbol of the world tree linking us to heaven above, to earth, and to the unseen underworld. Birch, often called the Lady of the Woods, offers nearly every part of itself as food. The bark feeds moose and white-tail deer when they find no other winter sustenance. Its sweet sap boiled down makes birch syrup. People found uses for birch in furniture, floors, and popsicle sticks. The bark is a shield against weather, the logs excellent for firewood. A first to grow from bare earth, birches birth the forest by beginning a fresh new resurrection of community. The white birch is on the vulnerable list in Indiana, imperiled in Illinois, Virginia, West Virginia, and Wyoming, critically imperiled in Colorado and Tennessee. In Canada the cherry birch is critically at risk. The trees are in danger of decline because their numbers are so few that the entire population's ability to reproduce is affected.

But the tree of life remains flourishing through all the generations of creation, omniscient with God's presence. A cherubim and a flaming sword guard the way to the tree of life. To have the right to eat from this tree and be healed by its leaves, we must become sanctified by taking shelter in God's fortress. We become flowing with living water, vessels absorbing his light, wanting others to understand his words. Needing more and more boldness to assure the children will take their place among God's gardens, those who speak are finding it less easy to grow new seeds on a land scorched by disbelief and mockery. "To the one who conquers I will grant to eat of the tree of life, which is in the paradise of God" (Rev 2:7).

The mouths of the righteous utter wisdom, and their tongues speak what is just. The law of their God is in their hearts (Ps 37:29–31).

The righteous will never be uprooted, but the wicked will not remain in the land (Prov 10:30).

2

SOUTH AMERICA

The fruit of the righteous is a tree of life, and the one who is wise saves lives (Prov 11:30)

In the sound of two words — Lord Jesus — campaigns unleash banning worship, guerrilla warfare turns its guns to silence prayer, fires are set to burn down churches, court rooms forbid speaking of sin.

All these are the beginning of birth pains (Matt 24:8).

Are we prepared?

The Pew Forum on Religion and Public Life finds that Christians are suffering persecution in more places today than any other religious group. Between 2006 and 2012, Pew reports believers in Jesus were targeted for harassment in 151 countries. Shifting with the spread of Christ's message, as much as 75 percent of persecution now occurs in the global south, according to the Religious Freedom Project at Georgetown University.[1]

A century ago forest blanketed 35 million acres of South America from the southern tip north into Chile and east into

---

1. Johnson, "Religious Freedom Project"

Argentina. The largest stands of earth's pristine rainforest flourish here. Felling the trees began with the arrival of European settlers in the sixteenth century, thousands and sometimes several million acres at a time. The shape of the landscape altered more through the 1950s as trees were replaced with a mono-culture of commercial eucalyptus and pine or used to pasture livestock.

Earth's 6 million square miles of tropical rainforest have shrunk to 2.4 million square miles because of deforestation.[2] All the plants, birds, bugs, and animals who give salutation to the tree are pushed to the brink of extinction. These are groves God's creative skill established to regulate the world's temperatures and weather patterns. Critical to maintaining our finite amount of fresh water, the rainforests harbor 75 percent of the 2,000 plants being used to treat cancer. These represent fewer than 1 percent of the rainforest's species being analyzed for medicinal properties. An entire pharmaceutical waits to be discovered.

By 1997 the International Union for Conservation of Nature Red List of threatened species presented an unprecedented loss of natural habitats and the species and ecosystems dependent on them.[3] The report verified nearly 34,000 species of plants, 12.5 percent of the world's flora face extinction. By 2006, the IUCN documented 23 plant species had gone extinct in South America and more than 8,000 were at risk of disappearing. Home to about half of all known species, the loss of rainforest is affecting lives of both those dependent on the trees locally and the rest of the planet.

South America is the fourth largest continent with 6.8 million square miles and beautiful islands including the Galápagos, Easter Island, and the Falklands. The equator passes through the continent bringing the Tropic of Capricorn where the daylight's sun remains high all year. The tallest point along the equator, Mount Chimborazo in Ecuador, rises as a sleeping volcano covered with glaciers that are mined for ice. The continent reflects centuries of colonialism in its racially, ethnically, and culturally diverse people

2. The Nature Conservancy, "Rainforest Facts"

3. International Union for Conservation of Nature, "The IUCN Red List of Threatened Species"

from Africa, Europe, and Asia. Marriages between Europeans and native people created the mestizo people of mixed ancestry who today comprise large portions of the population. Most of the 386 million people who live here are along the coastal regions, leaving the inland and southern regions sparse of human population.

Waterfall of the Deepest Place, known as Angel Falls, in the jungle of Venezuela is earth's highest waterfall. Cascading over the edge of the Auyantepui mountain, the water falls from 3,212 feet along the Gauja River. Indigenous peoples continue living in these regions as their ancestors had for thousands of years.

The demographic study of 200 countries by the Center for the Study of Global Christianity estimates the body of Christ today is 2.18 billion Christians of all ages among the world's 6.9 billion people.[4] The church has become truly global this century.

For as the soil makes the sprout come up and a garden causes seeds to grow, so the Sovereign LORD will make righteousness and praise spring up before all nations (Isa 61:11).

The study showed that in 1910 about two-thirds of the world's Christians lived in Europe where they had been for a millennium. But a hundred years later more than a third, 37 percent, are now in the Americas under attacks from neighbors, schoolmates, crime groups, and humanistic ideologies. One of four, 24 percent of the global body of Christ live in sub-Saharan Africa, and about one of eight are in Asia and the Pacific, comprising 13 percent.

Missionaries bringing the news of the Lord anticipate the attack that follows the message as they travel up in the Andes, earth's longest mountain range, bordered by the Pacific Ocean on the west and by the highlands and river basins on its east. They carry the words of Jesus out to the Amazon jungles, along tributaries into shanty towns. There are few roads. The word of God comes here by foot or motorcycles provided by Christian organizations.

Missionaries meet with local leaders who are familiar with the issues unique to the lives of each community. The aboriginal Christians bring the salvation to their people through holding

---

4. Pew Forum, "The Size and Distribution of the World's Christian Population"

outdoor meetings drawing crowds from among the tribes. Small local churches extend teachings to those in relationship with other villages and forge bonds with outside missions in a growing network. Preaching every Sunday, running a food program, helping with job training, those called to produce fruit that seeds the land here may be only miles from a paramilitary squad. The council of Evangelical Churches of Columbia reported forty Protestant leaders were assassinated in 2004 and more than fifty congregations forced to close because of the violence that has killed a quarter million Columbians since the 1980s. Deaths include sixty-two Catholic priests, nuns, and missionaries.[5]

The Amazon, spanning eight South American countries, drains into earth's largest river, the Amazon River. Earth's most diminutive deer live here among the trees, the southern pudu with buffy brown fur and sharp antlers. The pudu and its relative the northern pudu in the Andes are declining because of loss of trees to deforestation. On the endangered list their numbers rise and fall with the tree population. Home to a busy wildlife including jaguars, tapirs, monkeys, anaconda, vicuna and piranhas, the basin also sustains the populations of many tribal groups.

Isolated groups of indigenous people live unchanged by remaining separate from non-native societies and see missionaries as a tool of colonialism. An unknown number have not yet heard of Jesus. In 2013 the OAS Inter-American Commission on Human Rights released a study that found there are indigenous peoples in voluntary isolation or initial contact in Bolivia, Brazil, Colombia, Ecuador, Paraguay, Peru, and Venezuela. Their presence is also in Guyana and Suriname, near borders with Brazil. They are dependent on the trees for their survival.[6]

The modern world has been steadily closing in on their traditional lives of hunting and gathering, growing crops of rice and bananas. Amerindians make trips to towns to bring foods to

---

5. US Department of State, Columbia, "International Religious Freedom Report 2004"

6. Organization of American States, "Report: Indigenous Peoples Voluntary Isolation"

markets and purchase utensils but globalization of the market has been invading the Amazon with large-scale clearings for agricultural crops and pasture displacing their familiar sustenance.

Logging during the past three decades has brought death to hundreds of people in land wars, lives threatened by those who profit from the theft of timber and others who live in fear. It all began with a road splitting the Amazon along a thousand miles, known as the soy highway. Today every mile of more than 105,000 miles of roads is unauthorized, illegally built by loggers in search of the tall big-leafed mahogany and other hardwoods for export. In the past half century nearly 20 percent of the Amazon rainforest has been cut down. The loss left the slender-bill parakeet declining to the threatened species list. The south Andean deer have been driven from their forest by European introduction of cattle ranching. Woeful creaking as a towering life is severed from its source of strength echoes as trees like the bones of valiant soldiers lay fallen across the land. Now on the endangered list, the deer survive in small woodlands in southern Chile where the trees are low and gnarled by the ocean winds.

Never have we heard such groaning as earth's ecology unravels, persecution escalates, and creation yearns for the births of all God's children to be fulfilled. The worst earthquake in recorded history was a 9.5 magnitude that shook the planet on the Sunday afternoon of May 22, 1960, battering the coast of Chile with tsunamis, sinking a ship, blocking a lake with landslides, killing thousands of people, erupting a volcano, and caused a tribe to sacrifice a five-year-old boy in hope it would calm the earth. So strong, the quake shifted earth's axis and shortened daylight by a microsecond.

The Amazon's intricate design produces half its own rainfall by releasing its moisture into the atmosphere. Every month four to twenty inches of rain fall back, keeping it warm and wet year round. Cutting down the trees abandons the other trees, dry and dying. Along with the specter of a warming climate, drought could bring ravaging wildfires, lower the rivers and leave communities stranded. In 1998 more than 15,000 fires burned 2.2 million acres in Nicaragua, releasing carbon dioxide accelerating the greenhouse gases, and pushing rare species toward extinction.

Surviving for millions of years, the monkey puzzle evergreen has a wide range throughout the continent. A member of the conifers, the monkey puzzles are being logged for timber, displaced by development, cleared for cattle ranches and mining for silver, gold, iron ore, copper, petroleum, and tin.

Their crowns are interwoven atop a wide knobby trunk clothed in thick bark. The upper branches grow cones amid thick sharp leaves that release bright orange-brown seeds in the spring. The seeds lie dormant until the following spring when they germinate under a full blue sky, impassioned for the radiant energy of the sun.

Monkey puzzles benefit from lightning striking to remove trees that over-shade them. It gives the Malpuche people its nuts, similar to pine nuts, and their name, meaning People of the Monkey Puzzle Tree. For thousands of years the people did not exploit the trees. The trees were allowed to mature for the wind to pollinate. Some trees today began life as a seed 400 years ago, but commercialization has not left enough seeds to regenerate and its abundance is declining. In 2013 its status was listed Endangered by the IUCN.

Pau brasil that gave a country its name is also losing ground. The tree's dye is extracted from the heartwood, its bark studied for treatment of cancer, and its survival needed for the habitat of orchids. Large areas of forest were lost to extensive export of the dyewood. Local people were enslaved to do the work. The population of pau brasil declined rapidly with the spirit of hope in the enslaved people.

Found in the threatened Atlantic Coastal Forest of Brazil, the country with the greatest diversity of indigenous peoples living in isolation, the pau brasil grow among dry coastal cactus scrub, rocky outcrops, tropical forest, as well as sandy woodland. Traditionally the tree has given itself to making tools for the local people but today it is harvested to great loss for timber valued for making musical instruments, bows for stringed instruments, and exported for its heartwood. Pau brasil is on the list of Brazil's threatened plants. A reintroduction program for the tree at Linareas Reserve is hoped to restore its presence.

Evergreens from ancient times include the podocarps. Their straight unbranched trunks with dense needles supporting its place in the forest is disappearing this century. Listed as a threatened species on the 2006 IUCN's Red List, its plight brings government, NGOs, the United Nations, and companies together to develop best practices. Podocarp wood does not weather well and isn't sought for exterior doors or windows. Its use is for ceilings, floors, and furniture because of its light wood. Today we see its hard wood in butcher blocks because it doesn't chip easily.

The interior, unseen parts of the body of Christ create the fabric of the church community. Inside its walls is a lens to look out upon the world with Christ's perspective, doorways to come in and out, bringing others, finding shade, foundations to stand on, and restful chairs to let the members be still and listen. Other parts of the body take the seeds for new members to branch from the vine of Jesus. The brightly plumed leorie and rameron pigeon thrive on podocarp seed and help it scatter among other seeds. The tree grows where it is dropped and determines where the cape parrot live when they come search for the fruit's kernals.

The birds continue doing their work distributing seeds but urbanization is destroying the places soil sustains the ecology of South America. The rainforest is burning. Trees are clearcut to supply industries. Ranches and towns are displacing woodland, all of it increasing pollution into the Amazon basin. Reducing carbon emissions has become a priority in South America's participation with the 2009 international Copenhagen Accord, dependant on trees being able to fulfill God's design for them.

Their struggle summoned organizations around the world to take action. In November 2014 scientists, foresters, agronomists, indigenous peoples, and other experts from six continents met in Asunción, Paraguay to discuss problems of engineering the genetics of trees. On March 3, 2015 the international World Rainforest Movement, Global Justice Ecology Project, the Campaign to Stop

GE Trees, and Biofuelwatch held protests at Brazilian embassies and consulates in cities around the globe, including Wellington, New Zealand, London, England, Berlin, Germany, Ottawa, Canada, and Montevideo, Uruguay in opposition to the Brazilian National Biosafety Commission considering approval of GE eucalyptus plantations.[7] In Melbourne, Australia, protesters dressed as koalas, owls, and other forest creatures as they sought to prevent GE eucalyptus trees replacing nature's diversity.

The commercial development of genetically engineered eucalyptus trees would displace forest communities with one type of tree, causing loss of woodland communities, conflict over land, and removal of indigenous peoples. God's design bringing together diverse gifts of his people to serve as one body is being displaced by diluted teachings casting shadows on God's light and leaving the land absent of Christ's words. Christians here are in the midst of a civil war that's lasted more than four decades. In many regions guerilla, military, paramilitary, and drug cartels battle against each other without law to stop them. Civilians get caught in the middle if they offer an alternative through the redemption of Jesus. Believers in Jesus refuse to participate in drug dealing or violence against others. They stand for the thousands of farmers under attack by crime groups ordering them to grow drugs.

Because church groups won't pay protection money or be ordered by crime groups, pastors are being killed. Church buildings once a place of gathering to worship now lay in rubble. Church members flee into cities to be away from the rural areas. Congregants are being taken hostage. Open Doors World Watch List, an international aid organization, lists Columbia number thirty-five of countries where persecution of Christians was severe in 2014.[8]

> Then you will be handed over to be persecuted and put to death, and you will be hated by all nations because of me. At that time many will turn away from the faith and will betray and hate each other (Matt 24:9–11).

7. Campaign to Stop GE Trees
8. World Watch List, "Open Doors"

Those transformed into new creations by the pure light of God burgeon revival against the oppression, the way seeds burst through the cracks in concrete with faith's strength of joy.

> In all this you greatly rejoice, though now for a little while you may have had to suffer grief in all kinds of trials. These have come so that the proven genuineness of your faith—of greater worth than gold, which perishes even though refined by fire—may result in praise, glory and honor when Jesus Christ is revealed (1 Pet 6–7).

New Tribes Missions USA reports evangelicals growing at a rate of 6 percent a year in South America, three times higher than the rate of population.

As Christianity grafts people into the tree of life, cultural traditions are combining. People are interacting, sharing faith that's spreading into global tourism, investments, and knowledge about the land that sustains them. Indigenous societies are a strong presence focusing on sustainable resources and environmental legislation to honor their relationship with the wealth of lands. Christ is creating relationship out suffering that is bringing people to support and pray for one another and care for our trees.

Trees cannot move to other locations when problems come but God has designed helpers who come when a distress signal calls to them. Researchers from the Experimental Station of Arid Zones and the Netherlands Institute of Ecology discovered that the scent a tree emits to warn other trees of infestation also calls birds to flock to a tree infested with caterpillars.[9] The birds are attracted by scent emitted by damaged leaves. For the bird, the tree communication provides information about the presence of food, especially when birds have nests of chicks waiting to be fed.

Reports of the distress among those talking of the tree of life summon prayer. They say to each other be brave and believe. Bringing the light of the tender mercy of forgiveness, Russ Stendal was accused of being a terrorist leader as he worked among

---

9. Scientific News Service, "Trees Send Distress Signals to Birds When Attacked by Insects"

FARC to speak of Jesus.[10] Before a three-judge panel in Bogotá in March 2015, the Minnesota missionary was asked to explain visits into conflict zones to distribute Bibles and radios turning souls to look skyward toward the warming light. Chip Anderson, chief executive of Christ For the City International, said a trial of Stendal "would not only cause chilling effects on US missionaries, but also on national missionaries and churches." The alarm brought every mission to pray in one voice for the drop of water that began such a great mission to the deep roots, branching new believers, fostering seeds to spread new growth.

The December 18, 2013 Morning Star News reported an estimated 150 churches were forced to close in 2013 when the Front of the Revolutionary Armed Forces of Columbia People's Army (FARC-EP) forbid churches in the Putumayo state of southern Columbia.[11] Christians live in constant danger from an army that has banned worship in most small towns and villages. Only if permission is given by the rebels is a church allowed to meet without fear of violence. Those at highest risk are local churches and the visiting evangelists who serve them.

Prayer is continuous for leaders who go out to share Christ's message, never knowing if they'll make it home. FARC-imposed bans ordering churches to close, forbidding visits to outlying communities, or to teach the word of God have resulted in execution. A quarter million people have lost their lives in the half century since FARC launched its war, according to a study by Colombia's National Center for Historical Memory. Hundreds of thousands of families have been uprooted by the violence, becoming refugees.[12]

Because of the increase of wickedness, the love of most will grow cold, but the one who stands firm to the end will be saved (Matt 24:12–13).

---

10. Alford and Morgan, "Terrorism Charge Snares Prominent American Missionary"

11. Morning Star News, "Columbian Guerrilla Group Bans Worship Services and Threatens Pastors"

12. National Center for Historic Memory

We implore you on Christ's behalf: Be reconciled to God (2Cor 5:20).

To those who hear the word it is a seed handed to them, alive and growing. When the seed is planted there comes a time to shed its covering and unveil the source of the water of life. In Matthew 13 Jesus sits by a lake as the crowds gathered around him. He got into a boat and sat down out in the water. He spoke to the people on the shore about a farmer sowing seed. As he was scattering the seed, some fell along the path, and the birds came and ate it up. Some fell on rocky places, where it did not have much soil. When the sun came up, the plants were scorched and withered because they had no root.

Other seed fell among thorns, which grew up and choked the plants. Invasive species taking root on land they do not belong on, trailing along the ground to find a tree to wrap around, choking the gifts of God's design, act as our concerns overtaking us with worry for the approval of the world rather than of God. The rocks of guilt, disbelief, fear, or selfishness that hardens hearts had to be softened and porous so roots could grow deeply.

They made their hearts as hard as flint and would not listen to the law or to the words that the LORD Almighty had sent by his Spirit through the earlier prophets. This is how they made the pleasant land desolate (Zech 7: 12, 14).

Again and again I sent my servants the prophets, who said, Do not do this detestable thing that I hate! But they did not listen or pay attention; they did not turn from their wickedness or stop burning incense to other gods. (Jer 44:4).

They turned their backs to me and not their faces; though I taught them again and again, they would not listen or respond to discipline (Jer 32:33).

While you were doing all these things, declares the LORD, I spoke to you again and again, but you did not listen; I called you, but you did not answer (Jer 7:13).

Jesus said of the prophecies, "Blessed are those who hear it and take to heart what is written in it, because the time is near" (Rev 1:3). He said to follow him means "take up your cross." In

Romans 5 Paul speaks of unlocking heaven's treasure being full of joy because of our expectation to share in God's glory, not because of present circumstance. Suffering makes the joy of his promises evident.

"May the God of hope fill you with all joy," he says (Rom 15:13), because we can be confident that God will fulfill what he has begun in us. Joy remains, the second in Paul's list of descriptions of the fruit of the Spirit, because we have been given a view of God's long term plan and know that he is sovereign over every storm.

> "You rule over the surging sea; when its waves mount up, you still them" (Ps 89:9) "He got up, rebuked the wind and said to the waves, Quiet! Be still! Then the wind died down and it was completely calm" (Mark 4:39). "The Lord thundered from heaven; the voice of the Most High resounded" (2Sam 22:14). "And after these things I saw four angels standing on the four corners of the earth, holding the four winds of the earth, that the wind should not blow on the earth, nor on the sea, nor on any tree" (Rev 7:1).

Paul, chained to a guard, was desolate, yet filled with joy seeing the eternal work Jesus was accomplishing, planting seeds, watering the soil, watching with delight as new growth filled the land. He could see the branches increasing and the blossoming green leaves. Accepting God had planted him, he lets the water flow, the fruit grow, and speaks to the guards about the reason for his joy.

Rejoice and be glad, because great is your reward in heaven, for in the same way they persecuted the prophets who were before you (Matt 5:12).

The roots, trunk, and branches that represent a universal culture of protection, regeneration, and abundant fruit, work together to keep the tree alive. Exchanging nutrients and water, receiving sustenance from earth and light from the sky, they transform with strength to flower with fruits. Bound to earth, yet able to touch the sky, trees absorb the light for all life.

Jesus in the upper room with his disciples tells them, "These things I have spoken to you, these things they will do, so when the hour comes, you will be outcasts by those who think they serve God" (John 16).

Around the world groups gather in fear for their lives, risking imprisonment, fines, and threats because we are heirs to the prophets. But those who reject us are not what define us. God takes us in. Just as the creation began with light, man is transformed with light, brought out of the darkness. We are given our identity, taking on that stewardship to bring the message to the conscience of men until the end of the age. Some witness by their deaths. The world sees and considers.

Still other seed fell on good soil, where it produced a crop—a hundred, sixty or thirty times what was sown (Matt 13:8).

The soil had to be prepared. The seeds had to be watered. As rock is weathered by rain, freezing, thawing, and the winds, minerals become available to the soil to give to trees. Water drenches the ground and dissolves the minerals to move through the soils in relationship intent on nourishing the lives around them.

Nitrogen, abundant in our Milky Way, is strongly bonded so it does not react to pressure or temperature. Nitrogen is a building block to create growth. Phosphorous forms the membranes around cells to separate it from its surroundings. Found in minerals in earth, it forms the basis of DNA that creates the features of a life. If it's lacking, there are symptoms of malnutrition that weaken a life. Phosphorous governs the rate of growth and repairs wounded cells. It fosters bone formation with the strength that stands us up.

The soil adds to this with potassium necessary for living cells to function and do their work. Potassium ions diffuse for nerve communication. Its depletion in animals and humans results in various cardiac ailments. Potassium accumulates in the tree to infuse in fresh fruits to give to others and is important in maintaining water in the body.

When there's limited water in the soil, the leaves hold back by closing the stomato on the underside to keep in the moisture for the tree. Words don't come as abundantly as we wait to be watered, finding that God's plan provides unexpected helpers. Roots are colonized by fungi to help the root absorb more water and minerals to bring protection and growth. Leaves may be waxy on the surface, or rough, or paler colors to reflect heat and light.

A tree is worn, rough, scarred on the outside protective bark. Cambium cells layer new bark annually in response to the leaf buds at the ends of branches signaling a time to grow. The outer bark continually renews from within to protect from the environment, retain moisture, and insulate from heat, cold, and insects. The inner bark, sapwood, is the tree's pipeline for water moving up to the leaves. Sapwood lays new rings each year as old cells turn to heartwood. The heartwood formed within as if from songs and the words of God is untouched, the central pillar that supports the tree and does not decay or lose strength.

Today I have made you a fortified city, an iron pillar and a bronze wall to stand against the whole land-the kings of Judah, its officials its priests and the people of the land (Jer 1:18).

Therefore have I set my face like flint, and I know I will not be put to shame (Isa 50:7).

Bringing the words of Jesus enters us into a storm of opposition. The armor of God protects us with a belt of truth, a breastplate of righteousness, feet ready with the gospel of peace, a shield of faith, a helmet of salvation, and the sword of the Spirit (Eph 6:13–17).

Truth sanctifies with the words of God. A breastplate is fitted to the belt to shield our heart from accusations and hurtful words because we have a right relationship with God because of Christ. Our feet are prepared with the gospel of peace. "Peace I leave with you; my peace I give to you. Not as the world gives do I give to you. Let not your hearts be troubled, neither let them be afraid" (John 14:27). We are taught to recognize the enemy's strategy and become able to walk through the dangers. The footprints we leave along our path are confident with the truth of Christ.

We are able to stand when the "flaming arrows of the evil one" target us because we know our position is rooted in God's will. Holding a shield of faith, aware that God works all things together for the good of those who love him extinguishes doubt and splinters all false teachings. "Without faith it is impossible to please God." "Now faith is confidence in what we hope for and assurance about what we do not see. This is what the ancients were commended for" (Heb 11:1,2,11).

Because of faith, everyone born of God is given the helmet of salvation protecting our mind in the battlefield of false doctrine, emotional fears, and spiritual deception. To break through the enemy's shroud of lies and expose it to the light, the Word is described as the living, active sword of the Spirit, sharper than a double-edged sword. The Word is wielded by the Holy Spirit, requiring training for the soldier, "all of them wearing the sword, all experienced in battle, each with his sword at his side, prepared for the terrors of the night" (Song 3:8).

Without the truth of his words first belted around us, the other armor slips. With it, we are conformed to the image of Christ. "And pray in the Spirit on all occasions with all kinds of prayers and requests. With this in mind, be alert and always keep on praying for all the Lord's people" (Eph 6:18). The life flow of prayer waters all the world's trees to stand firmly rooted.

With this perfect design, the body of Christ is as diverse as a healthy forest. Each tree has its own variety of seed for propagating fruit.

> Then God said, Let the land produce vegetation: seed-bearing plants and trees on the land that bear fruit with seed in it, according to their various kinds. And it was so. The land produced vegetation: plants bearing seed according to their kinds and trees bearing fruit with seed in it according to their kinds. And God saw that it was good (Gen 1:11–12).

The alerce trees growing to great heights in South America are ancient, as old as 3,640 years, here before Jesus walked upon earth. Displaying its whorled leaves shading the laurel and myrtle, the alerce are considered to be the second longest living trees on earth, next to the bristlecone pine of North America and inspire the awe of its relative the giant sequoia. They are the largest tree in South

America. Wood found in Monte Verde suggests the towering tree has been used by people for 13,000 years. Its longevity gives science information about the changes in environment during its life. The new growth that the cambium adds to the tree each growing season creates the tree's memories in rings. Surviving a fire years ago, or plentiful water when it was young, the time it lost a branch, or the year when there was an insect outbreak are recorded here. The rings tell of struggling not to faint in a season of drought and convey stories about how people lived. Widened rings on one side of a tree tell how it strengthened itself during a hurricane that blew against it. These elders among the forests are like the elders among us who can tell us about what's happened, how the Lord helped them to survive it, and recognize the dangers around us.

The alerce produces fragrant cones containing two-winged seeds on its short branches. Appearing only intermittently across the land, its regeneration is compelled by volcanic activity or fire that brings it to leaf out to form acres of chlorophyll on leaf surfaces facing to the sun making food that brings the cycle of life.

Slow to reproduce, the alerce needs to grow 200 years to produce seed. Coveted for their lumber, they have been cut down in such numbers that few groves remain. Now highly endangered in Argentina and China, they continue to be illegally taken for the world's timber market.

Lord, see how my enemies persecute me! Have mercy and lift me up from the gates of death (Ps 9:13).

All your commands are trustworthy; help me, for I am being persecuted without cause (Ps 119:86).

If the world hates you, keep in mind that it hated me first (John 15:18).

Remember what I told you: A servant is not greater than his master. If they persecuted me, they will persecute you also (John 15:20).

Who shall separate us from the love of Christ? Shall trouble or hardship or persecution or famine or nakedness or danger or sword? (Rom 8:35).

However, if you suffer as a Christian, do not be ashamed, but praise God that you bear that name (1Pet 4:16).

God is our gardener carefully tending to the roots and each branch and bud. Jesus said, "If you remain in me and I in you, you will bear much fruit; apart from me you can do nothing. If you do not remain in me, you are like a branch that is thrown away and withers; such branches are picked up, thrown into the fire and burned" (John 15:5-6)." Attempts to grow without being rooted in God's design renders a barren landscape.

Your strength will be spent in vain, because your soil will not yield its crops, nor will the trees of your land yield their fruit (Lev 26:20).

God carefully waters the trees so that branches are alive and growing. "Whoever believes in me, as Scripture has said, rivers of living water will flow from within them" (John 7:38).

Ezekiel saw this water spreading out and deepening. In a vision recorded in chapter 47 he was brought to the entrance of the temple and saw water coming from under the threshold of the temple's east side where the temple faced. The water flowed down from under the south side of the temple. In the vision the man showing him this went east with a measuring line in his hand and led Ezekiel through the trickling water as it deepened to his ankles. As he led Ezekiel further through the water, it became knee-deep, then up to the waist. The water increased into a deep river that Ezekiel could not cross.

Ezekiel was asked, "Do you see this?" From the bank of the river he saw a great number of trees on each side of the river. He was told:

> This water flows toward the eastern region and goes down into the Arabah, where it enters the Dead Sea. When it empties into the sea, the salty water there becomes fresh. Swarms of living creatures will live wherever the river flows. There will be large numbers of fish, because this water flows there and makes the salt water fresh; so where the river flows everything will live. Fishermen will stand along the shore; from En Gedi to En Eglaim there will be places for spreading nets. The fish will be of

many kinds—like the fish of the Mediterranean Sea. But the swamps and marshes will not become fresh; they will be left for salt. Fruit trees of all kinds will grow on both banks of the river. Their leaves will not wither, nor will their fruit fail. Every month they will bear fruit, because the water from the sanctuary flows to them. Their fruit will serve for food and their leaves for healing.

Making pathways to the farthest valleys and highest mountains for the Lord's Spirit to flow over the earth with his glory, the words are shadowed at each step. But his words prepared us. Just before he walked into his dark night of Gethsemane, Jesus was concerned with what will come upon his disciples. Even as he faces separation from God such as none will ever experience, he prepares them. It will be upsetting. It will be terrifying. But, "never will I leave you. Never will I forsake you," he assured them. As he prays his last prayers, he says, "Now my heart is troubled, and what shall I say? Father, save me from this hour? No, it was for this very reason I came to this hour. Father, glorify your name!" Then a voice came from heaven, "I have glorified it, and will glorify it again" (John 12:27–28).

After he had prayed, Jesus was arrested. He was taken by the soldiers into the hall of Pilate where Roman soldiers gathered around him. Mocking him they stripped his clothes away, put a purple robe around his soldiers and pressed a crown of thorns onto his head. The holy one of God was silent as he was spit on and repeatedly beaten on the head so badly that he was barely recognizable. This had been prophesied. "His appearance was so disfigured beyond that of any human being and his form marred beyond human likeness" (Isa 52:14).

The ones who must kneel to the machete, stand in the courtrooms, be discriminated against, or fall under bullets, saying "not my will oh God but yours be done" leave us the glory of God.

All the trees of the forest will know that I the LORD bring down the tall tree and make the low tree grow tall. I dry up the green tree and make the dry tree flourish. I the LORD have spoken, and I will do it (Ezek 17:24).

Let justice roll on like a river, righteousness like a never-failing stream! (Amos 5:24).

Perhaps they will listen and each will turn from their evil ways (Jer 26:3).

But they would not listen (2Kgs 17:14).

3

EUROPE

> When you lay siege to a city for a long time, fighting against it to capture it, do not destroy its trees by putting an ax to them, because you can eat their fruit. Do not cut them down. Are the trees people, that you should besiege them? (Deut 20:19)

Melodies of birdsong, scented with pines supporting branches with bundles of green needles. Boughs hang heavy with hazel nuts and the oak's acorns towering over bushes ripe with blackberries offered to all who pass by. The woodland hums with the busy workers of insects accompanied by the wind whispers of leaves. Under its awning, the forest echoes in the human spirit asking, how are we connected to this community?

Europe was adorned with the hues of forest seasons, magnificent stands of elms, yews, ash, and chestnuts. When man asked for shelter the trees answered. When man was ill the forest replied with her raiment of wildflowers offering medicines. And when man wondered where to find wisdom the trees stood rooted to earth bridging to heaven with branches inspiring questions about celestial gifts.

Europe

The sixth largest continent, Europe's mainland is east of the range of Ural Mountains and encompasses isles of Iceland, the British Isles and many surrounding islands. Thousands of generations, through the ancient Greek and Roman civilizations to the Germanic tribes in the sixth century were sustained by the woodlands. The trees bestowed their staple of nuts, berries, cradles for the newborn, caskets for the dying, fire for warmth, and kindling to light the night. The abundance of wood supported Europe building ships to explore the world across rough seas. Trade and commerce extended relationship to other lands as the wooden ships navigated in along coastlines. The trees were so needed that Venice in the western Mediterranean consumed its timber by the fifteenth century and needed to import wood for ship hulls from northern Europe.

The Celtic people would leave a great tree in the middle of land cleared for settlement. It was the presence of the *Crann Bethadh*, Tree of Life, and stood a guardian axis, its sacred branches stretching to the doorway of the sky. A common Celtic knot called the tree of life symbolizes the unbroken dance of creation uniting heaven, nature, and humans to each other. Their enemies would triumph if they could cut down the tree, destroying the embodiment of the people's covenant with life.

Relationship with the trees inspired traditions and stories passed on to sons and daughters. Roots stretching out of sight brought thought of the unseen spiritual world and the ecology of creation's water in the depths of earth interacting with life to lift toward the power of the sky.

Converging at the start of creation and crowning its end, tree and water bring life.

> In the middle of the garden were the tree of life and the tree of the knowledge of good and evil. A river watering the garden flowed from Eden; from there it was separated into four headwaters (Gen 2:9–10).

> Then the angel showed me the river of the water of life, as clear as crystal, flowing from the throne of God and of

the Lamb down the middle of the great street of the city. On each side of the river stood the tree of life, bearing twelve crops of fruit, yielding its fruit every month. And the leaves of the tree are for the healing of the nations (Rev 22:1–2).

Water supports life. Its power can wear down mountains, build clouds, and reshape entire landscapes. Water carries seeds in streams and rivers, moistening the seed case and unlocking the growth within. Water brings life to the trees bordering hundreds of wells across Europe. Like temples where the ancestors were drawn together to drink and bathe, the waters carry memories beneath winds moving through the sheltering branches over us.

The water moves through the branches for trees to mark places to remember. "Now Deborah, Rebekah's nurse, died and was buried under the oak outside Bethel. So it was named Allon Bakuth" (Gen 35:8). They are places we are drawn to shelter. "So Abram went to live near the great trees of Mamre at Hebron, where he pitched his tents" (Gen 13:18).

Roots anchored in earth slow the rain and snow seeping in the soil. Where land has been deforested, storms strip the topsoil and choke the watersheds. Later when the season is dry there is no reserve. Without tree shade temperatures rise, killing fish and insects in the rivers. Without the leaves converting the sun's light into energy for the food cycle, entire species of plants and animals face the threat of extinction. The turtle dove, once thriving in the British country, is now vanishing. The 2012 census turned up the lowest count citing temperature changes causing droughts that wearied the land. Loss of trees changes culture and the way of life of peoples who give thanks to God for the well-being of trees supplying their survival.

Forests clothe 30 percent of earth's land. Europe's objective of limiting climate change to 2 C degrees requires cutting global emissions by at least 50 percent by 2050.[1] It will be possible only with the help of trees. Deforestation contributes about 20 percent of global CO_2 emissions.

---

1. Climate Emergency Institute, "2 Degrees Celsius"

If we lose our believers who stand in our midst, we will lose the workers who depend on them for the good news that redeems the lost and dying.

Europe has been considered a Christian culture influencing civilization for nearly 2,000 years, since the first century when Paul addressed believers in Greece and Rome. Sporadic local attacks of Christians took place throughout much of the first 300 years when Christianity was seen as a superstition and governors of each province had discretion to prosecute.

The days are again the days of Paul. In Turkey, the land the Hittites occupied north of present day Iraq, where the tree of life symbolizes the ancient faith of rebirth and growth of the Turkic peoples, songs lift in praise to the Lord even as stories pour into reports of fires burning churches and schools being attacked.

> Do not fear their threats; do not be frightened. But in your hearts revere Christ as Lord. Always be prepared to give an answer to everyone who asks you to give the reason for the hope that you have. But do this with gentleness and respect, keeping a clear conscience, so that those who speak maliciously against your good behavior in Christ may be ashamed of their slander (1 Pet 3:14–16).

In December 2014 Worthy News reported arsonists caught on security cameras set flame to the Correspondence School in Istanbul, a nation predominantly Muslim. The fire destroyed nearly half of the 40,000 books with smoke damage and the water used to extinguish the blaze. In March 2011 five military officers and two civilians were jailed for killing three Christians in 2007. The Christians, a German and two Turks, were tied up and their throats were slit at a publishing house in the southern city of Malatya.

The world is watching how much the people love Jesus and their hope is placed only in him. In Sweden a midwife was fired for refusing to perform abortions. In Hungary the European Court of Human Rights ruled that a law had violated the rights of churches and other religious groups by stripping them of state registrations, according to Barnabas Aid. Assist News Service reported about sixty Christians detained in Greece for distributing New Testaments in the Greek language. A woman in the UK had to argue in court to win the right to visibly wear a cross to work. A British family doctor in 2011 faced disciplinary action and risk of losing his job because he suggested faith in Jesus to a patient. In Germany in 2011 a Christian father was imprisoned for refusing to pay a fine for not allowing his children to attend government run sex education classes.

Jesus encourages disciples. "I have told you now before it happens, so that when it does happen you will believe. I will not say much more to you, for the prince of this world is coming. He has no hold over me, but he comes so that the world may learn that I love the Father and do exactly what my Father has commanded me."

In Phillippians 4, Paul who was harshly hunted down, experienced trauma, shaken by persecutions all around him, said to keep talking to God. "I know what it is to be in need, and I know what it is to have plenty. I have learned the secret of being content in any and every situation, whether well fed or hungry, whether living in plenty or in want." (v12)

We are to endure by walking softly along the paths God has designed through the forests where trees are secured with roots held firm in his will. Seasons of hail, winds, and thunders are in the palm of God's hands as a life marked by forbearance yields faith to others. This is what Christ did for us to bring us to do it for others. He reached out to those needing patience. He came to us accepting us as we are. "I was shown mercy so that in me, the worst of sinners, Christ Jesus might display his immense patience as an example for those who would believe in him and receive eternal life" (1Tim 1:16).

Forbearance enables us to patiently wait as the process of growth matures fruit for others. It is deliberate in its willingness to nurture. God's long suffering forbearance toward his wayward people patiently brings them back to him. Paul described the fruit of the spirit as singular, its yield listing God's qualities coming from his presence, beyond our inconstant emotions. Being rooted in the one tree of life is his heart. Modern society congratulates itself for its tolerance and acceptance of every type of person. Cultural norms change with the generations but the standards of God abide without end. Paul said, "If we endure, we will also reign with him" (2Tim 2:12).

Believers know that every plant not planted by God will be uprooted. When they speak to remind that Jesus is rooted in God's will and able to bring us the water of life, they are dismissed as small minded. Those who are left to thirst and mourn are lost, wondering who will lead them, because they're not being told about the promise of new life.

In a time when the cost of speaking could mean their lives, Paul and Timothy were confident that God's word could not be silenced. "This is my gospel, for which I am suffering even to the point of being chained like a criminal." But God's word is not chained. "Therefore I endure everything for the sake of the elect that they too may obtain the salvation that is in Christ Jesus, with eternal glory" (2 Tim 2:8–10).

The days of sorrow pass away, all things become new as the leaves blossom again to provide calm for the birds to nest. Supported by growth firm beneath the ground a tree's massive root system is not visible and rarely thought about. The sun patiently shines as roots steadily search for the water. In faith we patiently believe to see the budding shoot, confident in what we hope for and do not see. This faith comes from hearing the word of God (Rom 10:17).

A mature oak tree will send down a taproot and branch out hundreds of miles of roots, merging with other oak trees to anchor each other when the strong winds blow, even grafting to share a root system. Once rooted in a lifetime source of nourishment the tree produces branches and foliage. The threat to the oak tree's health is pavement compacting the soil and trenching for utilities or construction causing poor drainage that could smother and begin to rot the roots.

When a tree does fall we are not abandoned to a world of suffering. The light among the fallen remains in the seed so that there will be fathers, mothers and youth who don't despair and don't bend to the ides of social change. Encased in the safe, tough shell of each acorn is a single seed dependant on birds and other animals to carry it away to an area where it can grow into a new oak tree.

As seeds emerge under threats of persecution, song clear and worshipful crack the hard covering, and like an acorn, splits open and the shell is shed. A new tree is in the heart of every seed shared with a new believer.

After an Islamic extremist group attacked the synagogue in the Danish capital of Copenhagen in February 2015, more than 1,000 Muslims formed a Ring of Peace around the Oslo synagogue to offer symbolic protection to the Norwegian Jewish community.[2] Holding signs saying "No to anti-Semitism, no to Islamophobia," they linked arms with Jewish community members. The turnout broke down walls and brought together people in the shared hope for peace. Dozens of peaceful Muslims visited the synagogue in Copenhagen to express condolence and create an alliance against the fanaticism that is drawing away the young, the angry looking for purpose.

Each tree brings its gift, an observance that inspired the earliest form of Irish writing, the ogham alphabet. Dating from about 4 AD, the alphabet is a series of lines and notches using trees and plants as letters, including the ash, pine, yew, birch, willow, alder, holly, hazel, and oak to mark borders and memorials.

Oak trees were subsistence, a pattern of survival that gave acorns to process for food through the ages. More than 500 species of butterflies and moths depend on this tree. In the presence of conflict the oak stands to heights of sixty feet with associations of thousands of years crowded around it. The tree lives more than seven centuries reminding of ancestors who once walked the land and endured the seasons under its awning. Its bark offers plentiful tannin, a strong astringent. Places in Ireland are named after the oak tree, "*dair*" which is also the origin of the word door in the

---

2. Associated Press, "1,000 join Muslim ring of peace outside Oslo synagogue"

Irish language. Kildare is known as "*Cill Dara*" in Irish, translated means church of the oak. The word Druid is considered a derivative of *dair*, meaning oak-seeing, through the doorway into past and future, earthly and heavenly.

Christianity came to Ireland by the early fifth century and spread through the works of early missionaries. It came with prohibitions against being Irish in the 1300s in British owned areas trying to eradicate their identity. In the 1500s Henry VIII outlawed the Irish language and took groups of English speakers to influence identity by relocating them in Gaelic plantations to dispossess the land, bring England's plants and flowers, and kill the wolves into extinction.

Five centuries later in northern Ireland, November 2014, Ashers Baking Company was court ordered to pay compensation or face legal action when the Equality Commission found the business guilty of committing "unlawful religious, political, and sexual orientation discrimination."[3] Their offense was in declining to bake a "gay" cake, according to Christian News. In May the bakery had been asked to bake a cake featuring a homosexual advocacy group logo in observance of the International Day Against Homophobia and Transphobia. Management declined to bake the cake because same sex relationship is against the company's Christian beliefs. The manager of the business, Daniel McArthur, said, "We are Christians and our Christianity reaches to every point of our lives." The customer, demanding respect yet not giving respect to another's belief, reported the Ashers to the Equality Commission of Northern Ireland who sent a warning to the bakery.

Accommodating a world wandering away from God shuts the heaven's rains. Left in drought, those struggling and brokenhearted won't hear Christ's words to save their lives. "For I resolved to know nothing while I was with you except Jesus Christ and him crucified," Paul said, and they imprisoned him for it. Yet the words he spoke reached countless millions through the generations who followed through the gateway of the redeemed.

---

3. BBC News, "Gay cake row"

Jesus said "small is the gate and narrow the road that leads to life, and only a few find it." The doorway is Jesus. There are fewer in the world that speak his truth, and many who walk the broad path accepting the world's ever-changing standards, unlike Daniel who purposed in his heart that he would not defile himself while others conformed.

Jesus said to the one who knocks, the door will be opened. Jesus receives anyone who calls to him. But he tells them it is a hard uncompromising road wrought with trials that will separate us from this world.

At least there is hope for a tree: If it is cut down, it will sprout again, and its new shoots will not fail (Job 14:7).

Among Europe's tallest trees, the ash is able to re-sprout and start growing again after it has been cut down. Roots safeguard us through the attack, bringing the source of living waters to renew branches full of leaves every new season. Every autumn trees show us the need for a new generation to rise, roots pushing their way through darkness, coming up against rocks, continuing unstoppable in their quest for the water.

Above their crowns the thunders carry the sound of God with lightning electrifying the air. Spring rains pour across the mountains, drenching meadows, streaming water down the land, draining into the deepest places to soften the soil and break down minerals into the soil, rich in elements to support the land's design for what will grow. Moses said there needs to be a first and a latter rain before there can be a harvest. Through Moses the people were told to faithfully love the Lord and serve him with all your heart and with all your soul "then I will send rain on your land in its season, both autumn and spring rains, so that you may gather in your grain, new wine and olive oil. I will provide grass in the fields for your cattle, and you will eat and be satisfied" (Deut 11:13–15). The nation was to keep God's words to be a great nation of wisdom and understanding.

When God was angry at the people for wandering away, Zechariah spoke. "Ask the Lord for rain in the springtime; it is the Lord who sends the thunderstorms. He gives showers of rain to all people, and plants of the field to everyone" (Zech 10:1). God would strengthen, restore, and they could pass through the sea of trouble.

The rains prepared the soil and Christ's words spread seeds that took root and reproduced more seeds showered to bring fruits of forbearance. The latter rain waits for the fields' triumphant harvest which belongs to the Lord "having a golden crown on his head and a sharp sickle in his hand. And another angel came out of the temple, crying out with a loud voice to him who sat on the cloud, Put in your sickle and reap, for the hour to reap has come, because the harvest of the earth is ripe" (Rev 14:14–15).

Be patient, then, brothers and sisters, until the Lord's coming. See how the farmer waits for the land to yield its valuable crop, patiently waiting for the autumn and spring rains (Ja 5:7).

The fruit of the Spirit brings the forbearance (Gal 5:22). We may need patience to wait for the unseen growth of a root system as a tree readies for harvest. Forbearance is needed through changing weather as we wait for the ash tree's black buds to bloom into lovely purple flowers. It's one of the last trees to put on its springtime leaflets then shed its winged seeds onto the forest floor to feed the wildlife. Growing slowly, it becomes strong flexible wood made into furniture, walking sticks, and sports equipment. With gray brown bark furrowed with diamond patterns, the ash belongs with the oak and hawthorn trilogy of sacred Irish trees. It is a tree of rebirth, taken to America with immigrants escaping the Great Hunger in the 1800s. Ash is a protective tree, used to make oars and coracle slats to carry us across deep water.

I tell you, my friends, do not be afraid of those who kill the body and after that can do no more (Luke12: 4).

Jesus warned that if the world hated him it would hate us too (John 15:18–20). All who would try to be godly will be persecuted (2Tim 3:12) and enduring the suffering will conform us into the likeness of Christ (1Pet 1:6–7). It was a time when the first believers faced much rejection socially and financially, inside their families and in their communities because they professed their faith. Realizing the long term plan of God, James spoke, "Consider it

Our Trees of Life

pure joy, my brothers and sisters, whenever you face trials of many kinds, because you know that the testing of your faith produces perseverance. Let perseverance finish its work so that you may be mature and complete, not lacking anything."

The hope is not that this life will change. Believers keep speaking because of the expectation of Jesus returning. Paul said the whole creation is in travail waiting for the manifestation of the sons of God. Tornadoes, typhoons, earthquakes, poisoned waters, trees falling, animals, birds, and fish struggling to hold on, all of creation groans together in this hope. It's the moaning of birth pangs giving new seeds of longing for Jesus to redeem. The Holy Spirit groans in an appeal to the church to hold fast and to listen, with warnings in the book of Revelation speaking of losing the first steadfast depth of love. Fear of suffering, compromising God's teaching, moral erosion, and failure to keep the faith through the growing opposition threaten every believer.

Jesus left these words with a mandate to read the signs of a world changing its attitude toward his body of believers. "I tell you, whoever publicly acknowledges me before others, the Son of Man will also acknowledge before the angels of God" (Luke 12:8).

Again and again God's word tells us to listen.

Listen, my dear brothers and sisters: Has not God chosen those who are poor in the eyes of the world to be rich in faith and to inherit the kingdom he promised those who love him? (James 2:5).

Therefore let it be known to you that this salvation of God has been sent to the Gentiles; they will also listen (Acts 28:28).

After three days they found him in the temple courts, sitting among the teachers, listening to them and asking them questions (Luke 2:46).

So Eli told Samuel, "Go and lie down, and if he calls you, say, 'Speak, Lord, for your servant is listening.'" (1Sam 3:8).

Parched and weary from the constant barrage against our faith, the heart calls, "Oh, that I had the wings of a dove! I would fly away and be at rest" (Ps 55:6). The Lord replies, "My Presence will go with you, and I will give you rest (Exod 33:14).

Do not be afraid, little flock, for your Father has been pleased to give you the kingdom (Luke 12:32).

Entwining knots in Celtic Europe denote the desire for faith, unity, and protection. They represent our innate yearning to express the eternal without beginning or end, the trinity knot representing the three ages of a woman, the love knot loops an unending bond, the sailor's knot woven in memory of unbroken love for ones at home, and the shield knot to signify prayers for protection. The Celtic spiral knot is still seen around grave sites, representing the journey from physical to spiritual being.

A triple spiral was knotted as a symbol between the interconnecting flow between land, water, and sky. Inspired perhaps by the enchanting flow of water beneath its branches as it watches over all who sit beneath it, the willow tree stands witness to our dependence on God continuing these interactions.

> He took one of the seedlings of the land and put it in fertile soil. He planted it like a willow by abundant water, and it sprouted and became a low, spreading vine. Its branches turned toward him, but its roots remained under it. So it became a vine and produced branches and put out leafy boughs (Ezek 17:5–6).

Willows inspire dreams in early displays of spring leaves on branches hanging low bending gently in the wind. The branches are pliant enough to allow tears and grieving. Hebrew people mourned their captivity in Babylon by the groves of willows. Yet the branches are also strong enough to weave into baskets to carry heavy burdens and support more than 400 species of butterflies and moths. Its bark contains salicin, used to treat rheumatic fever.

On the first day you are to take branches from luxuriant trees—from palms, willows and other leafy trees—and rejoice before the Lord your God for seven days (Lev 23:40).

Around the world plants and animals are changing the land in response to human activity causing trees to march toward the north, yet the expression of human longing they symbolize remains constant in its cry to God. In Europe there are butterflies sixty miles further north of their average range. Species such as the red fox and the checkerspot butterfly have moved northward with the trees. Salmon are found further north. Birds are laying eggs and migrating an average five days earlier than in the early twentieth century. New problems are afflicting trees as warfare mounts against Christ's words.

In May 2013 residents of the UK were asked to spot the oak processionary moth and ash dieback disease that were attacking trees.[4] A national survey was being taken to identity the presence of devastating caterpillars that could kill thousands of the trees across the land, including the hazel, hornbeam, sweet chestnut, birch, and beech. The caterpillars came into Britain on infested imported trees. First found in 2006, they strip the leaves from the trees in such large numbers that the oak is fatally wounded. The people were called out in hope to contain them in the areas already infected so that the trees could continue their gifts.

To assure us of God's worthiness, we are given a promise that will stand through all the changes still to come. His promise is in his words that we are to display, like leaves bejeweling a tree. If they are stopped from renewing, the tree will die and the entire community dependant on the light it absorbs will vanish. Speaking of Jesus as Lord of all, sovereign and absolute in his teachings brings the label of being intolerant or bigoted in a world trying to be proud of being politically correct. But the world sinks in the darkness, cutting down believers who are falling into God's hand. Another will rise up from the seeds of his words and begin to grow. The covenant promise has assured the growth will cover the earth.

They will be called oaks of righteousness, a planting of the LORD for the display of his splendor (Isa 61:1,3)

Let the trees of the forest sing, let them sing for joy before the LORD, for he comes to judge the earth (1Chr 16:33).

Standing alone on a hillside or greeting us at the edge of the forest, the hawthorn's roots reach into ancient stories. A small tree in the rose family, it blooms dark green leaves before boasting clouds of fragrant flowers of five white petals that inspired rites of fetching the May into villages to celebrate the return of the green

---

4. Gray, "Toxic caterpillar warning as infestation of oak moths spread"

growing earth. The little flowers become an abundance of small bright berries that birds and small animals feed on as autumn turns its leaves to yellow.

Hawthorn sprouts quickly to provide a tangle of impenetrable thorns. The thicket provides a protective boundary for nature's birds and animals to find sanctuary. The more it is pruned or nibbled at, the thicker the hedge grows. In Old Testament times a hedge of dense thorn bushes would be grown around a pen, protecting animals from predators as God protects us with his commands that prevent dark thinking from devouring us.

Being challenged in our faith begins the assurance that our roots will be firm until the end.

The pruning we undergo in the process stimulates new growth as God uses our struggles to develop thicker armor. The prophets searched for this light to see the path of salvation. Discounting their own discomforts and the mockers enclosing their lives, they prized passing along the knowledge above all else. They felt God's pleasure when they acted in accord with his desire for people to know him.

The Spirit of the Sovereign LORD is on me, because the LORD has anointed me to proclaim good news to the poor (Isa 61:1).

It's been said that the crown of thorns Jesus wore was made from the hawthorn tree. To the ancients their hedge symbolized the boundary between the familiar physical world and the unknown forest beyond, a gateway to the spiritual mysteries. Growing in Europe, North America, Africa, and Asia the people everywhere used it for the same medicinal remedy to treat cardiovascular disease. The flowers, leaves, berries, and seeds work to strengthen each other to dilate blood vessels, regulate blood pressure, and stimulate the muscle of the heart to have a strong pulse. The tree's gifts improve peripheral circulation to all parts of the body.

Winter rustles through the branches telling the trees to drop their leaves so water can be retained as the sky darkens and the light becomes less. Chemical breakdown of the green chlorophyll reveals the orange and yellow colors in the carotenes and xanthophylls. The scarlet colors are enhanced by hard frosts affecting residual sugars and anthocyanins. The ash will be the first to drop leaves. The oaks, ironwood, and beech may hold onto brown leaves well into winter.

With leaves as with man, the busy work for God is dependent on the light of a star. When God handed the ten commandments to Moses, he began by reminding that he is the God of deliverance. He spoke instructions that would light the protections of the family unit with honoring the mother and father, being a faithful spouse, committing no harm against another person, and renewing our presence in our relationship with God. In concern that the people remember the words, Moses wrote them down and warned that God would hold accountable anyone using his name to commit wrong teachings. Underlying a culture where God's words are not woven into the moral foundation, where all truths are considered acceptable, there is no light of God. The trees intended for righteousness stand dormant.

I chose you and appointed you so that you might go and bear fruit (John 15:16).

Thriving on the abundant full sunlight, pioneer species that begin to re-grow a forest spread out their branches and shade the forest floor. The other trees follow, the beech, hemlock, mountain ash, hazel, and dogwood under its canopy. The birch's seedlings wait with patient stillness under the shade of the forest floor, unable to thrive without the full sun.

The birch is one of the earliest to display spring leaves, bringing thought of driving out the old year and renewing again an agricultural year. Birch live more than a hundred years growing white bark as it matures. Bright green alternating leaves and flowering greenish white catkins droop clusters from branches. From the tips of its twigs flowers are wind pollinated, dropping seeds through the fall and winter. The birch is the first tree to sprout among the ferns after a fire has decimated an area. The tree provided paper, canoes, baskets, and maypoles symbolically the earth's axis we turn and turn around. Because we'd have pain in this world, the birch offers relief in its bark and arthritis treatment in its leaves.

In Wales wreaths of birch are woven as a symbol of enduring love. In Russia it is the tree of life. Windowsills are adorned with its branches and girls wear birch woven into crowns. A tree is adorned with ribbons, beads, herbs, and flowers, carried by girls and young women around the fields and down the streets as they sing songs of earth's renewals. Walking in a grove of birch is said to lift the spirit, touching the birch's white bark reduces stress. The tree gave paper, footwear, crafts, tents, and inspired art to the Slavic people. With its crown touched by heaven, the tree is known as a keeper of truth and knowledge, with roots that bring water to the everyday needs of life.

Above the trees of winter, bright burning fireballs entered earth's atmosphere just after sunrise on February 15, 2013, streaking across the sky. People of Russia felt its intense heat. The meteor exploded in a loud flash of light eighteen miles overhead, trailing smoke as blast waves damaged thousands of buildings and left pieces of meteorites strewn on the snow covered ground.[5]

"There will be great earthquakes, famines and pestilences in various places, and fearful events and great signs from heaven," Jesus prophesied.

For the first time the US Commission on International Religious Freedom placed Russia on the list of concern.[6] People who receive funding from outside the country are classified as foreign agents. In the eastern Ukraine Orthodox militants destroyed churches, kidnapped pastors and tortured and killed them.

Blessed are the dead who die in the Lord from now on (Rev 14:13).

In Russia today a church can meet if it has the government's permission but there can be no independent Bible study or evangelizing. In January 2015 two Kazakh Christian men were fined for worshipping in a church without the state's permission.[7] When they refused to pay their fines, Nikolai Novikov was banned from leaving the country. Maksim Volikov, who was also fined for evan-

---

5. Space.com, "Meteor Blast Over Russia"
6. US Commission on International Religious Freedom, "Russia"
7. DeCaro, "Two Christians Fined by Kazakhan courts"

gelizing in a village without permission, had more than 165 books, magazines, and CDs confiscated. Maksim had been fined before for forming a church group in his house. Artur Alpayev, a Christian in Uzbekistan, was fined after religious literature was seized from his home during a raid by police in August 2014. The judge said the literature has to be stored in a building belonging to a registered religious organization. Artur's Christian group refuses to seek state registration despite the flood of efforts to uproot them.

The birch is easily uprooted by rapidly moving water. The graceful delicate tree shows us the still waters that we are led to find. At times the Lord will make us lie down and be still in his pastures. Barricades and obstacles may surround us as we are taught to "Be still before the Lord and wait patiently for him; do not fret when people succeed in their ways, when they carry out their wicked schemes" (Ps 37:7) or else we'll be uprooted.

In this world you will have trouble. But take heart! I have overcome the world (John 16:33).

The birch reproduces by growing from its rhizomes, seldom from seed. Its mass of roots forming underground send out and nourish new shoots that will grow upward into new trees. Even if a rhizome becomes split into pieces, each part could rise into a new tree. If the tree dies, the growth of its roots has assured the fruits it offers will continue.

Autumn brings clusters of hazel nuts wrapped in green leafy shells, sustaining generations of birds, animals, and people. Gathering outside in the fresh air the people picked the nuts as the cattle were led back down from summer's upland pastures and a community festival marked the beginning of winter. Throughout the countryside the leaves feed livestock, its branches build fences for safety, furniture for rest, and firewood for warmth. The leaves may fall but the fruit of the nuts bring vitamin B6, thiamine, vitamin E, proteins, magnesium, iron, and potassium. They lend themselves to salads, grind up for flour to bake bread and pastries, flavor coffee, or are eaten freshly cracked.

Known as the Irish nut, the dependable properties of strength and health the hazel nuts bring contributes to the tree being known to give wisdom and inspiration. A legend tells of hazel trees growing around a pool of water at the mouth of the Boyne and Shannon rivers. The trees dropped their nuts into the water and a salmon ate nine of them, each representing a kernel of wisdom. When a druid teacher caught the salmon, a boy named Fionn MacCumhail cooked the fish, tasted it, and absorbed the poetic sweet knowledge contained in each nut. He became a hero. Reminding every generation to appreciate relationship between the tree, the water, the salmon, and a person, the story of the hazel tree, known as *bile ratha* (venerated tree of the ringfort) continues being told.

The hazel provides shade because we will need rest, protection because we will not always be safe, and baskets because our Creator instructs us to carry each other's burdens and continue to bear his fruit.

Another legend tells of the Oak King of summer battling the Holly King of winter to tell of the vigor of nature's balances as seasons wax and wane. The holly is traditionally burned as a Yule log to mark the end of winter's reign. Holly is esteemed for withstanding severe winters and still bloom its four petal flowers. When bitter winds blast the land burying gardens and hedges under deep snow, frosting the windows and dripping icycles from every rooftop, the holly stands radiantly green reminding the world the coming spring is worth fighting for.

In the upper room before Jesus goes to the cross he spoke to his disciples of peace in his comments in John 14. "Do not let your hearts be troubled. I go and prepare a place for you. I will come back and take you to be with me. You know the way to the place where I am going."

We have come to share in Christ, if indeed we hold our original conviction firmly to the very end (Heb 3:14).

4

AFRICA

That person is like a tree planted by streams of water, which yields its fruit in season. (Ps 1:3)

Silhouetted on grasslands, the baobab tree rises to an impressive eighty-foot height with branches of hand-shaped leaves forming a wide roof. Hornbills, parrots, and kestrals make their nests in the hollow trunks. Eagles find welcome in the boughs. Vultures and storks come to raise their young.

The smooth gray bark around the baobab's girth can grow to forty feet round to create a cistern storing hundreds of gallons of water inside the trunk, bringing it to be known as Africa's tree of life. Strong root systems go deep in dry regions to sustain the animals and people with fruits, seeds, and oil. Its leaves and flowers feed wildlife and strengthen the immune system. Fibers from the bark are used to make rope and cloth.

Some of the baobab trees standing today have been here for more than a thousand years sheltering the people from the lightning that brings torrential downpours in the rainy season, fitting a dozen people inside as the broad leaves shed the rain and slow the winds.

The continent boasts earth's longest river, the Nile, flowing northward through the largest of all deserts, the Sahara, on its way to empty into the Mediterranean Sea. Millions of tons of nutrient rich sands from the desert cross the Atlantic Ocean every year to dust the jungle floors of South America's Amazon, replenishing phosphorous the Amazon depends on because it loses so much to rains and floods.

The equator passing across the middle of Africa brings tropical weather to the fifty-four sovereign countries that occupy earth's second largest continent. One billion people live here, about 15 percent of the world's population. The oldest fossil evidence of human beings has been found here.

The highest rates of murder occur in Africa, according to the United Nations 2014 Office on Drugs and Crime.[1] The study reported nearly half a million people died from intentional homicide in 2012, 36,000 of them children under fifteen. The study cites 6.2 per 100,000 as a global murder rate, but South Africa recorded more than four times that, at twenty six victims per 100,000 population, a drop from the 64.5 per 100,000 reported in South Africa in 1995.

The land is etched with conflict. Two fronts are attacking Christians in Nigeria. The Fulani militants want land and Boko Haram want an Islamic State. The IS in Iraq and Syria (ISIS) has penetrated into all of North Africa fueled by disputes over borders, natural resources, and the war on terrorists. Believers carrying the message of Christ, like Nigerian Pastor Joshua Adah, are at continuous risk of being caught in the crossfire.[2] Joshua was traveling to villages during his evangelistic outreach bringing medical care, clothing, and the message of Jesus. Coming back to the village of Bantaje on January, 23, 2015, Joshua's vehicle broke down and he was killed by Muslim Fulani herdsmen and members of Boko Haram. He left behind his wife and two children ages six and eight.

1. United Nations Office of Drugs and Crime."World Drug Report 2014"
2. Smith, "Nigerian Pastor Butchered to Death"

For 2,000 years the message of Christ has given rise to a faith that separates from race, color, and nationality that every generation discovers anew. The new interpretation of God quadrupled the number of Christians around the world in the past century, according to the Pew Research Center's Forum on Religious & Public Life's 2011 Global Christianity: A Report on the Size and Distribution of the World's Christian Population.[3] But the population has risen too, from an estimated 1.8 billion in 1910 to 6.9 billion in 2010, leaving the percentage of Christians still about 32 percent of the world's people.

The shift of faith is in geography. Europe and North America were once home to 93 percent of Christians in 1910, the majority of the world's believers. The Pew report found a much lower number of believers in Europe and America in 2010, dropping to 63 percent of the world. During those years Christianity has grown most steadily in Africa and Asia where there were few Christians at the beginning of the twentieth century.

In sub-Saharan Africa, the number of believers climbed from 9 percent in 1910 to 63 percent in 2010. Jesus has created a global neighborhood and with it a brand of faith targeted by persecution. The growth of faith in African countries brought the largest increase in persecution in 2014, according to Open Doors, especially in sub-Sarahan Africa. Djibouti moved up from the forty-sixth country of most concern in 2014 to twenty-fourth in 2015, the second biggest leap after Kenya. Sudan, where Meriam Ibrahim was imprisoned, sentenced to death, and later released to find asylum in the US[4] rose from number eleven to number six. Worthy News estimated Nigeria's 158.2 million people are comprised of 51 percent Christians and 45 percent Muslims. Murders and kidnappings of Christians pushed the West African nation to the top ten places of the worst tyranny on earth in 2015, rising from fourteenth in 2014.

---

3. Pew Forum, "The Size and Distribution of the World's Christian Population"

4. Marshall, "The War on Christians"

The trees continue on the land storing water for streams in the desert as they always have, sustaining life as Christ's presence grows. In Kenya where sycamore figs stand like queens along river banks, a young university student, George Muriki, stood at the gate of a church building in Mombasa on January 11, 2015 and was mistaken for the church's pastor. An unidentified man approached and shot George three times in the back.

In Nairobi, Kenya, students at Garissa University College were awakened at dawn on Thursday, April 2, 2015 by the sound of bullets being fired in one of the school's six dormitories.[5] Five or more gunmen stormed the guards, killing them. They shouted, "*sisi ni al-Shabab* (Swaihi for we are al-Shabab)," as they mercilessly fired into the building, shattering glass in a fury of bullets whistling through the air as they asked students, "Are you Christian or Muslim?" With each answer of "Christian" a blast of gunfire killed a student. Other students were held hostage. Police and military officers surrounded the area as al-Shabab snipers atop a three story dormitory shot at them. The AFP reported the attack took the lives of 142 students, three police officers, three soldiers, and wounded at least sixty.

Outside where students once sat talking with friends, trees stood in the sun offering shade. Local residents gathered beneath the branches to donate blood for the wounded. When the massacre was over, police and soldiers stood under the trees to find a moment of quiet. Inside, books were left scattered on the floor in puddles of the blood of those the Islamic extremists had taunted. Shoes and pens dropped and left behind in hallways lay silently abandoned.

Out along the rivers giraffes feed on the leaves of the sycamore fig and a pair of gray hornbills find home. A new sycamore begins its life as a seed helped by tiny fig wasps who live only hours to do this important work. The wasp must enter a fig through the bud's gate where thousands of flowers are harbored. The tiny wasps transfer pollen from one flower to another. Here she leaves her

---

5. Botelho, "Kenya's Garissa University College awakens to Islamic militant terror"

eggs protected until they are ready to carry on the job as the figs ripen and grow heavy. When the cycle is done, the tree sheds its leaves. The wasps depart and the fruits feed more than a hundred kinds of birds who fly in from miles away to celebrate this gift. Bats come to suck the juice and disperse the seeds in a wide area for new trees to grow. People come and use its branches to build a fire, smoke out bugs, and gather a rich honey.

The small gate for the wasps to enter the flowers transforms a seed into the shelter of a towering tree inviting every people of every nation. On the night before Jesus was crucified, he told his disciples that he would be leaving them. He assured them saying, "My Father's house has many rooms; if that were not so, would I have told you that I am going there to prepare a place for you? And if I go and prepare a place for you, I will come back and take you to be with me that you also may be where I am" (John 14:2–3). The Greek word for rooms meant "family." Jesus was telling his disciples that in God's heaven there is a plan to gather from the many families of peoples of the world, "a great multitude in heaven that no one could number" who all would be welcomed by the tree of life.

Let no foreigner who is bound to the LORD say, "The LORD will surely exclude me from his people." And let no eunuch complain, "I am only a dry tree" (Isa 56:3).

To produce more fruit from God's tree, Jesus grafts in more branches. There must first be a rooted tree, the first born who made possible the water of life to be shared into the branches so that the fruits will belong to the same tree. The branch that will bring buds is taken and whittled deeply into the green layer of growth, joined to the tree and covered with the outer protective bark to unite the cambium layers together to share one source.

Isaiah tells us that those who share God's Sabbaths and hold fast to his covenant will be given a memorial in his temple, better than sons and daughters. God will give them an everlasting name that will endure forever. Foreigners who bind themselves to the Lord to serve in his work will be brought to his holy mountain.

They will have joy in God's house of prayer. It will be a house of prayer for all nations.

The Sovereign LORD declares—he who gathers the exiles of Israel: I will gather still others to them besides those already gathered (Isa 56:8).

As the steady march against our souls follows into Africa, the Voice of the Martyrs reported that on January 2, 2015 homes were torched and fifteen people killed by Fulani militants in the Kaduna State. Ten others were murdered on December 27.[6] In the Plateau State, Fulani gunmen murdered three Christians on New Year's Eve, beheading one of them. A suicide bomb attack in the Gombe State injured eight Christians guarding a prayer service on New Year's Day.

Worthy News reports from 2014 tell of Fulani herdsmen from a border town attacking villages in Nigeria's Benue State to kill five Christians and destroy homes and churches in December.[7] The Islamist herdsmen and their mercenary allies had killed and maimed Christian villagers for months making life unbearable.

Heaven's Light Church in Harare, Ethiopia, was demolished on November 28, 2014 by order of the Shenkore administrative district that just days before had forcibly removed the church's sign.[8] Sudanese Police broke through the main gate of the Khartoum's Bahri Evangelical Church, arrested and fined each of the thirty-eight Christians $250 in December 2014.[9] The worshippers were charged under Article 77, which allows Sudanese authorities to arrest minorities for "creating a public disturbance."

On October 19, 2014 armed Muslims wearing military uniforms stormed two churches in Taraba State and killed thirty-one Christians as they worshipped. The slaughter of the two pastors and twenty-nine others was the seventh attack on Christian

---

6. Voice of the Persecuted, "Christians Killed"
7. DeCaro, "Islamic Herdsmen Again Attack Christians in Benue, Nigeria"
8. DeCaro, "Ethiopian Officials Destroy Evangelical Church"
9. Morning Star News, "Police in Sudan attack worshipping congregation, arrest 38 Congregants"

communities in eight months. Islamic insurgents killed 1,631 Christians in Hiberia during the first six months of 2014.[10]

In 2013 1,783 Nigerian Christians were killed for believing Jesus.[11] Barnabas Fund's October report of the leader of the Boko Haram broadcast the abduction of more than 200 school girls in April from Borno State in Nigeria, forced to convert to Islam and married off to Muslims. That same month the Sudanese Air Force dropped four bombs on a church in the Nuba Mountains in the South Kordofan State. Fulani Muslims destroyed a church in Plateau State killing ten Christians that September.[12]

Beginning their life already in defeat, who will stand silhouetted in a landscape of endless persecution and contain the presence of living waters in a land of drought?

When the rain holds back and the soil becomes dry, the trees are struggling and all of life will struggle too. Severe drought in Africa delayed red-backed shrives and thrush nightingales as they lingered to find enough food to make the rest of their journey through buffeting storms and violent winds across the Mediterannean Sea to reach the trees where they will sing again.

Trees in every country are disappearing from the land, falling to disease, toxins, non-native insects eating away their hearts. Trees bring our breath. A mature tree exhales oxygen for ten people to breathe. They cleanse the soil and prevent erosion so that there can be water for all life.

Blessed is the one who stays awake and remains clothed, so as not to go naked and be shamefully exposed (Rev 16:15).

The lonely journey of a messenger for Christ is given winds of promises to lift him. He knows that he will sing again when he completes his work. It may seem that the wicked have won. The violence is paralyzing locals who depend on outside services

---

10. Morning Star News, "Muslim Extremists Kill 31 Christians in Taraba State, Nigeria"

11. Barnabas Fund, "Boko Haram reveals fate of abducted schoolgirls, continues atrocities in Northern Nigeria"

12. Evangel.fm, "Sudan Air Force Bombs Church Complex in Nuba Mountains"

for health and education. Fear keeps many away from teaching at schools or ministering in a targeted region. As with the early church who withstood torture and death so that we would have the knowledge of Jesus, God's believers again are being pushed underground as the darkness takes up rule. God's enemy sheds the blood of the prophets and kills the watchman of God. But they still cannot silence God's words.

Those who have stood under the attacks on Christ's mercy seat cut short the growth of a choking vine that can root bitterness when we see our world's condition. They know they will rejoice over the fate of anything that inflames against Jesus. "Rejoice over her, you heavens! Rejoice, you people of God! Rejoice, apostles and prophets! For God has judged her with the judgment she imposed on you" (Rev 18:20).

No longer will they build houses and others live in them, or plant and others eat. For as the days of a tree, so will be the days of my people (Isa 65:22).

The baobab blooms for the first time after growing for twenty years. It brings gourd-like fruits hanging from long stems off the branches. Inside the fruit is a nutty powder that can be mixed with water to make a velvety nutritious drink with three times as much vitamin C as an orange and more calcium than spinach. The fruit can be used for making porridge as well as the leaves, which can be used in a salad.

Europe's appetite for the fruits of Africa are consuming the baobab's gifts faster than the trees can grow. The UK based Natural Resources Institute estimated that the trade in baobab's pulp fruit could be worth up to $1 billion a year for African producers, employing more than 2.5 million households across the continent.[13] But to be sustainable the tree needs people to start growing more trees now.

Many afflictions have placed the baobab tree on the endangered list. Drought has left them without enough water. Striving to survive, people have cut down many of them to use the trunks to store rain. The tree's fruits are full of seeds, from its Arabic name

---

13. Baobab Superfruit, "Ethical Trade and Sustainability"

wor bu hibab, meaning fruit with many seeds. Some of these seeds are eaten by elephants who break the seed dormancy to cause regeneration. The population of the elephant is also endangered and the baobab trees continue a decline.

Destruction of the world's trees affects every land. Each continent's forests serve the balance of the entire globe. According to the UN between 1950 and 1980 Africa rapidly lost 23 percent of its forests.[14] A cascade of problems followed with flooding, loss of soil, and deserts encroaching. The savanna of southern Africa is changing as rising levels of carbon dioxide in the atmosphere push trees to grow over the grasslands working to balance the air. An acre of trees may use 5,880 pounds of carbon dioxide and give back 4,280 pounds of oxygen for all of creation to breathe. The plains of the Serengeti, the woodlands of the Kruger National Park, and the dry red sands of the Kalahari comprise more than half of the lands south of the Sahara Desert. Cycles of rainy seasons and brush fires in dry seasons are accelerating woody plants displacing the extensive grasslands.

Driving the change is greed, the compulsion to rule and conquer, all the elements that satan tempted Jesus with in the desert. Because Adam in the Garden of Eden ate from the tree that gave mankind a desire to follow their own knowledge, death came. But Adam did not eat of the tree of life.

This would be for Jesus to bring us so that in him we will still have life after the unfruitful works of darkness, the galls, disease, the axes that cut down the Spirit's fruit, are ended.

It is used as fuel for burning; some of it he takes and warms himself, he kindles a fire and bakes bread. But he also fashions a god and worships it; he makes an idol and bows down to it (Isa 44:15).

He prays to it and says, "Save me! You are my god!"(v 17).

Our wilderness moment tempting us to choose another way may last only a heartbeat as the decision is made to remain a branch grafted into God's will. When the Israelites were surrounded by oppressions, the defeat of their enemy began, "After

14. United Nations Forum on Forests, Tenth Session

consulting the people, Jehoshaphat appointed men to sing to the LORD and to praise him for the splendor of his holiness as they went out at the head of the army, saying: 'Give thanks to the LORD, for his love endures forever'" (2Chr 20:21).

The praise prepares the soil, the hardened stony hearts have been plowed. The ground is softened and our compassions see the world around us through Christ's eyes. "Your fruitfulness comes from me," God reminds (Hos 14:8). The fruit of the Spirit brings kindness (Gal 5:22). Jesus said when you gave a glass of water to the thirsty, clothes to the naked, comfort to the imprisoned, it is the Spirit's fruit. God calls people from fruits of darkness with kindness.

"Brothers and sisters, if someone is caught in a sin, you who live by the Spirit should restore that person gently" (Gal 6:1) Kindness understands the struggle. "Be kind and compassionate to one another, forgiving each other, just as in Christ God forgave you" (Eph 4:32).

After being beaten then hung in the morning light, nails pounded into him, Jesus looked out on all of humanity in the kindness of his holiness. "Father forgive them. They do not know what they are doing." The sky darkened. He was placed in a tomb and it appeared that his enemies had triumphed. The angels in heaven waited. Then the sound never before heard exalting his promised victory began unfurling across earth, rising in every language on every land and in every rhythm of music. The message instructed to rejoice with those who rejoice; mourn with those who mourn (Rom 12:5).

African women, guardians of the children, managing food resources, water and education, are burdened now with the developing world demanding them to survive through the labor force. Increasing their work load, taking them away from their central role in the family's well-being, the shift against women has left them vulnerable to violence and separated from relationship to God providing for her through the land.

The World Health Organization found millions of women in Africa are suffering violence.[15] Fifty-percent of women in Tanzania and 71 percent of women in Ethiopia's rural areas were found beaten by husbands or partners when a 2005 study was done. Amnesty International reports a woman is killed every six hours in South Africa. In Zimbabwe six of ten murder cases in 1998 were related to domestic violence. In Kenya in 2003 the attorney general's office of domestic violence accounted for 47 percent of homicides. The violence extends to female genital cutting that can cause infection, childbirth difficulty, and death. It includes forced marriages, forced pregnancy, forced abortion, forced sterilization, trafficking, and forced prostitution. The women work the land or bring in wages all their lives only to be left without land, alone, and empty.

Where are the trees to shelter them?

The trees will yield their fruit and the ground will yield its crops; the people will be secure in their land. They will know that I am the LORD, when I break the bars of their yoke and rescue them from the hands of those who enslaved them (Ezek 34:27).

Animals like the cheetah are suffering as open country savanna becomes filled with woodland from what is termed the CO_2 fertilization effect. The savannah separates the deserts from the tropical forests near the equator. Giraffes thrive on the leaves of the acacia trees that grow scattered with the baobabs across the savannah. Climate shifts are projecting to transform this into desert and strand the giraffe without sustenance.

The women of Africa need the quenching water of God's Spirit as shifting persecution covers their land.

God demonstrates his care for all his creation through water. He set in motion a cycle for water evaporating into the atmosphere to return to us as rainfall to quench the land. Water is stored in the oceans, rivers and lakes, held by trees, frozen in glaciers, or moving through underground aquifers. The atmosphere around earth contains water from the world's bodies of water, holding the heat so life doesn't freeze. Precipitation of rain, snow, sleet, hail, fog, and dew sends nearly 90 percent of the cycle to fall back into

---

15. Kimani, "Taking on violence against women in Africa"

oceans and the rest falling on the land to define the distribution of plants and animals. The trees hold many drops of water in their leaves and participate with higher rates of evaporation. The water in the ground transpires through root systems to above ground where the sun can lift it back into the cycle. One tree can help transpire a hundred gallons of water in one day to cool the atmosphere. All of life depends on this cycle.

I will send you rain in its season, and the ground will yield its crops and the trees their fruit (Lev 26:4).

When humanity produces the fruit of God following his precepts of wisdom, even the animals are well.

Do not be afraid, you wild animals, for the pastures in the wilderness are becoming green. The trees are bearing their fruit; the fig tree and the vine yield their riches (Joel 2:22).

To help regenerate the baobab tree, a group known as Practical Action has come together to save the species before its gift of water and sustenance vanishes. They collect and plant seeds, raise awareness, and encourage others to treasure baobab trees as well.

In the Western Cape Province the fragrant clanwilliam cedars grow to majestic heights standing in the mountains for a thousand years. Needing three decades to produce seeds, the cedar is also on the endangered list because since the eighteenth century its growth has been disrupted by extensive exploitation for building, furniture, and telegraph poles. Brush vegetation grows in the spaces and has been blocking the regrowth of the tree. Logging the cedar was banned in the twentieth century but the trees have been unable to recover because of fires. To support its survival a Cedar Reserve has been created to provide land for the trees and plant seeds to encourage their presence.

The women need a season of renewal so they won't grow weary and lose heart.

The blackwood tree comes up quickly, producing large numbers of seeds that disperse widely through successive stages of growth. Younger trees trying to fill their place in creation are threatened by the increasing man-made bush fires clearing land for agriculture but when they are able to mature they are a protective border resistant to fire. The tree is classified as Near Threatened and feared its scarcity could become extinct within a few decades. The African Blackwood Conservation Project founded in 1996 to cultivate young trees to replant where it has disappeared as well as establish school programs in Tanzania to increase local conservation awareness.

The women of Africa need the body of Christ to support those who minister under heavy persecution.

From a rough gray trunk the blackwood spreads branches adorned with clusters of sweetly scented tiny white flowers in season. Vital to the savanna's ecosystem, its roots fix nitrogen to produce fertile stable soil. The blackwood's modest presentation conceals a valuable heartwood, the supporting pillar of the tree, sought after by the entire world for its beauty and durability.

Heartwood is bound together by lignin making it as strong as steel through the blowing winds and falling rains. The wood was used by Egyptians for artifacts in tombs. It's used by the indigenous people to make utensils and intricate carvings that bring in revenue from tourists. It gets formed into woodwind instruments and preferred for making clarinets for the tone it produces. The blackwood is a musical tree, wanted to make guitars, drums, ukuleles, violin bows, and organ pipes.

The women and the persecuted of Africa need music. An unfaltering song of worship rises triumphant over dark clouds of pain.

The mosaic of trees from the tundra to the alpines continually reorganizes its design. The forest floor has experienced a long history of human presence. Settlements passed through, from hunter gatherers sustaining their families on the rich foliage and fruits of the trees, to small plots of farming that burned areas to clear for planting, to large populations that would collapse under disease then recover again. Higher populations today are found across western Africa and the north and east of the Congo with lower numbers in the central regions. As the world population burgeons, land use for cropland is expanding. The state of Rondônia in western Brazil is one of the most deforested parts of the Amazon. Two percent of its rainforest had been cleared by 1978. Thirty years later the trees had been felled on 34 percent of the land.

From the perspective of humanity the patience of nature for succession to regrow a landscape seems to take a long time. Influences of wind, fire, insect infestation, and logging alter how each member of the forest community grows. Combinations of trees define what abundance radiates around them. There may be a hundred common species or only a few that are rare, all interacting as a community. It may be the flock of birds at a lake shaded by trees or it may be a rotting log hosting bugs and moss. Under the crown cover animals, seeds, birds, fauna, and flora have safe routes for relationship, finding foods, birth places, and sanctuary from a predator.

The exploited victims need pathways created to connect them to others who carry the message of encouragement and hope.

Africa is the site of about 11 percent of the world's deforested regions. Half the continent's animal species find home in Africa's rainforests. The mountain gorilla maintains its 600 pounds on the lush vegetation. African elephants feed on the plentiful fruits. Monkeys find homes high in the moist broad leaves of thousands of trees that stretch for miles. Parrot squawking continues because of the sustaining fruits the forest grows. The smallest of hippopotamus species, the pygmy hippos, stroll between the trees.

Scattered and pushed away with nowhere to go, deforestation, roads and clearing for farming wiped out about 90 percent of West Africa's rainforests. In Central Africa's Congo, the Amazon rainforest, the world's largest rainforest, came under axe after centuries of being disturbed only by groups of native subsistence people. But in the nineteenth century when European loggers and plantation owners moved in, the rainforest fell.

The heart of Africa is an interworking of ecological, climatic, and human disruptions. Growing populations and war refugees have left governments conflicted between the need to protect the rainforest and the need for jobs that foreign logging companies bring. In 1999 six countries of the Congo Basin pledged to balance forestry with logging and poaching laws. They created the tri-national Sangha Park as a refuge to heal the thinning of the forest's ability to promote relationships that sustain life. Trees are taking time to recover. Emergent relationship is growing from a common root as they listen to each other in shared concern. Without the understanding of long term needs, many would be left to thirst.

The Amazon receives about eighty inches of rain every year with changes in rainfall causing changes in the growth. It is now one of the world's most threatened ecosystems. More than 8,000 plant species grow here thriving in the humid shadows. Ingredients for medicines are continually being discovered here. About 600 tree species grow in the rainforest, about 70 percent of the plant life, including coconut trees and the tall kapok tree. Twenty-five hundred species of vines grow here.

The land is layers of emergent, upper canopy that is so dense pouring rain landing on the leaves can take ten minutes to drip through to the ground, and the understory where the small bladder nut evergreen grows from Western Cape along the mountain slopes and shady lowlands up to Ethiopia. The bladder nut tree brings flowers that hang down as they develop into red berries encased in a calyx. The seeds are roasted as a coffee. Bark extract is used to treat cramps. Leaves and roots are infused to soothe skin rashes.

The afflicted of Africa need the medicine of comfort and told that because Jesus has put us here to sow seeds, he will return again at harvest.

Elephants, primates, and predators have been pushed toward extinction leaving empty forest in West Africa. Trails that created spaces once made by the animals fill in with plants and young trees, growing denser in the now silent forest. Ongoing logging trails into the rainforest intensify the consequence bringing hunters who take the survivors. Climate models indicate African rainforest regions will warm and not all tropical organisms will be able to adapt. Others have adapted to change for millions of years and are expected to continue. Eastern Africa is anticipated to become wetter. Madagascar may become dryer because of sea surface warming converging along the coast.

The rainforest's vulnerability depends on how trees are protected now. Each tree brings appreciation of a gift. The small rock alder is the first to reclaim injured ground, giving beauty for ashes with a mighty force of budding hope. Delicately straight, its trunk offers timber resistant to borers and termites. Little green and white flowers bring sweet scent as they mature into ripe fruits enjoyed by birds and animals. The bark is distilled into astringents and used to treat inflammation. Grounded, it has been an ingredient in toothpaste. Leaves are heated in bags and placed on arthritic joints.

Ironwood evergreens growing along South Africa's coast and up on the hillsides adorn themselves with sprays of tiny white flowers maturing into dark fruits, members of the olive family. Seeds carpet dry forest floors and wait years for the canopy to open and let sunlight in and winter rain to bring their growth. One of the tree's common names, "pock ironwood" comes from the dots along the central veins of the leaves. Inside the little pock marks microbes live symbiotically to keep the leaves clean of debris and mold.

Another evergreen, the hard pear on the Cape Peninsula grows from young smooth gray bark into rough reddish scaly bark as it becomes an elder of the woodland. A profusion of small white flowers become red berry fruits. Every part of the tree is scented. When crushed it releases a smell of almonds that is used as incense.

The women of Africa need to be clothed with fragrance that is the incense of Christ's love and realize he has given them gifts that they can bring to others.

> The fragrance of your garments is like the fragrance of Lebanon. You are a garden locked up, my sister, my bride; you are a spring enclosed, a sealed fountain. Your plants are an orchard of pomegranates with choice fruits, with henna and nard, nard and saffron, calamus and cinnamon, with every kind of incense tree, with myrrh and aloes and all the finest spices. You are a garden fountain,

a well of flowing water streaming down from Lebanon (Song 4:11–15).

To God, unlocking each gift in each seed is important to his plan. One person's transformation into a kingdom that has no borders matters more than conquering a nation. It is eternal. It is universal with each individual rooted in the type of soil and land where God has planted them. He is building his kingdom "so that no one may boast before him" (1Cor 1:29). God's choice of the weak vessels of the world to confound the mighty is purposeful. Reflecting the prophet's words, "Let not the wise boast of their wisdom or the strong boast of their strength or the rich boast of their riches" (Jer 9:23), we are to remember that God alone is our strength and source of living waters.

Hear me, my people, and I will warn you— if you would only listen to me, Israel! (Ps 81:8).

My sheep listen to my voice; I know them, and they follow me (John 10:27).

When armies of enemies were plotting war against Jehoshaphat and his people, "Then Jehoshaphat stood up in the assembly of Judah and Jerusalem at the temple of the LORD in the front of the new courtyard and said: 'LORD, the God of our ancestors, are you not the God who is in heaven? You rule over all the kingdoms of the nations. Power and might are in your hand, and no one can withstand you'" (2Chr 20:6). "Our God, will you not judge them? For we have no power to face this vast army that is attacking us. We do not know what to do, but our eyes are on you" (v12).

This is what the LORD says to you: Do not be afraid or discouraged because of this vast army. For the battle is not yours, but God's (v15).

5

ASIA

They made upright frames of acacia wood for the tabernacle.
(Exod 36:20)

Tu'B'Shevat, the New Year for Trees, is a time in Israel when the rains have fallen and the blossoms begin to appear on almond trees. The nuts are eaten to celebrate Tu'B'Shevat acknowledging God's righteousness in his faithful relationship with his creation.

Tu B'Shevat is the fifteenth day of the Jewish month of Shevat, beginning at the setting of the sun and continuing until the next day's sunset. Sometimes the day is marked by eating from the bounty of *shivat haminim* (seven species)—wheat, barley, grapes, figs, pomegranates, olives, and dates described in the land of Israel (Deut 8:8). The foods have held significance since ancient times, offering wholesome recipes for soups, salads, and desserts that bring spiritual connection to our Creator and physical alertness to learn the teachings of God. The Tu B'Shevat in 1890 began a movement to plant trees in the agricultural colony of Zichron Yaakov and was continued by the Jewish National Fund in the 1900s to restore the land of Israel. More than a million Israelis continue to participate in tree planting events on this day.

The holiday has become a day of ecological awareness entwined with Jewish values of *tikkun olam* (repairing the world), *tzedek* (justice), *g'milut hasadim* (kindness), and *shalom* (peace). It acknowledges times of waiting for growth, maturity, first fruits that belong to the Lord, and how there is always to be provision for the poor.

Celebrating a New Year for Trees was inspired by the Torah's teachings.

> When you enter the land and plant any kind of fruit tree, regard its fruit as forbidden. For three years you are to consider it forbidden; it must not be eaten. In the fourth year all its fruit will be holy, an offering of praise to the Lord. But in the fifth year you may eat its fruit. In this way your harvest will be increased. I am the Lord your God (Lev 19:23–25).

Tu'B'Shevat brings reflection on all the generations who were stewards of the earth and allowed a tree to strengthen its root system before harvesting its fruit. The book of Genesis goes on to tell us that man and woman were placed to be responsible in the Garden of Eden "to cultivate it and keep it" (Gen 2:15). Cities built in the Promised Land were circled with a perimeter of trees (Num 35:4). Fields of harvest are to lie fallow on the seventh year to regenerate rich soils (Lev 25:3–4).

We are to partner with God in the care of the land.

Asia covers about 9 percent of earth's land. It is the largest of continents, offering home to an estimated 4.3 billion people. Generations ago the continent broke apart from Africa, the Red Sea poured between the two lands, and ancient civilizations grew to become a center of world economy with oil countries of Saudi Arabia and Kuwait, manufacturing centers of India and Japan and banking headquarters of China. The Pew Forum December 2011 report counts Asia's 13 million Christians as the lowest concentration of believers in the world, about 4 percent of the whole.

ASIA

On the shores of the Mediterranean Sea in western Asia, Israel supports a collection of landscapes from the north's Mount Hermon alpine slopes to the south's Gulf of Eilat where colorful fish swim among coral reefs. An arid desert lies between, crossed for miles until stands of trees come suddenly into view, gathered as if families of ancestors lined up waiting to welcome home the weary, lonely traveler. According to the 2011 report of the Central Bureau of Statistics, the population of Israel is 7.9 million.[1] About 76 percent are Jews, 19 percent are Muslims, 2 percent are Christians, and 1.6 percent are Druze. The remaining 1.4 percent are small communities of Bahais, Samaritans, Karaites, Jehovah's Witnesses, and persons who identify themselves as Jewish but do not meet the Orthodox Jewish definition the government uses for civil procedures. Most non-Jewish citizens are of Arab origin. About 95,000 residents are foreigners on work permits.

The bible details the beauty of dozens of trees in the land of Israel, cedars on the snow-covered mountains of Lebanon, palms feathering their tops over clusters of dates in Sinai's desert oases, olive and fig trees outside the walls of cities, terbinth, aspens, pines, and ash standing in splendor on the land of the Hebrew people.[2] Sea-trading nations once stripped the cedars of Lebanon to build their ships. These are the cedars there for King Solomon to build the first temple in Jerusalem. Twenty-eight generations later, "When Jesus entered Jerusalem, the whole city was stirred and asked, Who is this?" (Matt 21:10).

"The glory of Lebanon will come to you, the juniper, the fir and the cypress together, to adorn my sanctuary; and I will glorify the place for my feet (Isa 60:13).

The cypress provided a way to sail upon the flood when God instructed Noah, "Go make yourself an ark of cypress wood; make rooms in it and coat it with pitch inside and out" (Gen 6:14). The ark today waits with patience for all who belong to God to be born as it lifts us in the rising flood surrounding his believers.

1. The Central Bureau of Statistics (Israel)
2. Jewish Reconstructionist Community, "Trees of the Bible"

Acacia trees are the foundation of life in desert places, sheltering hundreds of gazelles in their shade. The foresight of God created the tree to unfold small leaves to help conserve water and clusters of white flowers that bring fruit in pods containing several seeds. Porcupines, red foxes, desert larks, warblers, and shrikes are helped by the tree and in turn spread the seeds to grow. The roots fix nitrogen in the soil for the plants gathering around them. Bees are kept alive by the pollen and beetles depend on the pods. Bats find their most important habitat among the acacia.

The acacia's slow growth hardens the dark reddish heartwood where the tree deposits preservatives to resist decay and repel insects. It is the wood God instructed Moses to use to support the infrastructure of the tabernacle in the wilderness, taken from the desert's gnarled trees where the Israelites had wandered for forty years. The ark and its poles, the table and its poles, the alter and its poles, and the incense alter and its poles, created a place to bring people together to worship and remember God. The poles were used to carry the ark of the covenant when the people moved. The enduring tabernacle was used for four centuries and found rest in Solomon's temple in Jerusalem. The ark is again seen in Revelation after the seventh trumpet sounds. "Then God's temple in heaven was opened, and within his temple was seen the ark of his covenant. And there came flashes of lightning, rumblings, peals of thunder, an earthquake and a severe hailstorm" (Rev 11:19).

To acknowledge heaven's design in a symbolic way on earth, an offering the children of Israel could bring for the tabernacle was acacia wood. "Those presenting an offering of silver or bronze brought it as an offering to the Lord, and everyone who had acacia wood for any part of the work brought it" (Exod 35:24).

Sycamores grow in Tel Aviv, fig trees in Emmaus, and in springtime oak trees flower on Mount Tabor. The pines budding all across Israel were brought by the Jewish National Fund in the twentieth century because it can thrive on dry lands. The flowers of the olive follow in April and May. The cypress was planted as a border to protect orchards from wind. Poplar trees, hawthorn, and Jericho balsam tower everywhere.

ASIA

These are the trees that Peter knew, that Paul knew, and all the believers who first carried the message of Christ. Their lives too ended sadly, tragically. Paul was so cold and alone he asked Timothy to bring him his cloak. He left behind those who they had invested in, taught and prayed with who deserted Paul. Demus, who "loved this present world" left for a city that was a trade route of materialism. Demus saw the price Paul was about to pay and he departed the faith, loving the world more.

This is where the tree grew that was used to crucify Jesus. No one knows what kind of tree it was, how many years it grew under the sun or what birds nested in its branches before it was cut down, fashioned into a cross, and pushed into the ground. The seeds of that tree continued because, "They triumphed over him by the blood of the Lamb and by the word of their testimony; they did not love their lives so much as to shrink from death" (Rev 12:11).

On February 17, 2015 NPR reported tears streaking the faces of people in a small farming Egyptian town, el-Aour, a hamlet on the Nile south of Cairo.[3] Screams and weeping were heard from every house and street. The Islamic State had beheaded twenty-one men. Armed with guns, they drove four vehicles into a village the week before, sought out Christians, beat them, cursed them, and tied their hands behind their backs. Thirteen of them were from el-Aour where relatives bowed their heads in prayer.

A caption on the video IS released reads: "The people of the cross, followers of the hostile Egyptian church." It showed the solemn quiet in the faces of the men as they were marched in line to a beach and forced to kneel, a wind stirring their hearts as leaves of each promise of God were given to the watching world. One man lifted his eyes to the sky as he waited to die. Others closed their eyes in silent prayer. A witness heard one speak, "Oh Jesus," certain that the savior would be the next he saw and the higher court of God would judge this moment.[4]

Jesus in the throne room of heaven watched, his armies of angels gathering.

3. Fadel, "ISIS Beheadings in Libya Devastate an Egyptian Village"
4. Dean, "The ISIS war against the people of the cross"

Every tear will be redeemed.

Then each of them was given a white robe, and they were told to wait a little longer, until the full number of their fellow servants, their brothers and sisters, were killed just as they had been (Rev 6:11).

The population of el-Aour is about half Muslim, half Christian. Thirteen of the men beheaded came from el-Aour, prepared speak we would not realize we've been adopted into this warfare or know the promises before we can withstand the unfolding prophecies.

> Do not be afraid, Jacob, my servant, Jeshurun, whom I have chosen. For I will pour water on the thirsty land, and streams on the dry ground; I will pour out my Spirit on your offspring, and my blessing on your descendants (Isa 44:2).

The Aral Sea, a glimmer of water between Kazakhstan and Uzbekistan in Central Asia, was once the fourth-largest lake in the world. Now scarcely 10 percent of the sea is left.[5] The sea left behind the hulls of rusting ships, the death of fish, and hungry communities living in fields covered with layers of white salt where once melons and crops were harvested to bring to market. In the 1960s, the Soviet Union built dams and canals to divert the Syr Darya and Amu Darya rivers that flow into the Aran Sea to use in cotton fields and agriculture. Over the years the Uzbek cotton fields swallowed up all the water. The rain stopped. Grass dried and withered. Herds of antelope that once roamed here disappeared.

As the sea shrank, the fertilizers, pesticides, and insecticides used in the cotton fields washed into it becoming more concentrated. North-easterly winds blew across the dry sea, picking up the sand, salt, and toxins, and carried it far beyond the region to drop it on other places. Croplands were coated in salty dust and needed more water to be flushed.

The Uzbek government turned its focus to restore the balance to the ailing lands and people. Like the global community of

---

5. Golovnina, "Glimmer of hope for shrinking Aral Sea"

believers forging unity out of the persecutions, trees were found to grow together to protect the lives in their environments.

They designed a plan to plant the rugged saxaul trees on the seabed to reduce toxic salts from spreading. The trees grow extensive root systems that stabilize the soils. Several organizations joined in with planting trees around surrounding cities in 2011 to prevent the dust from spreading. Now the sky gazes on the beauty of May greening the fruit trees that will bring an annual harvest.

Damage to a tree will lead to changes in nearby trees too. An injured leaf radiates the change toward the trunk and throughout the tree. Waves of defensive chemicals surge from the tree regulating the passage of charged ions. The leaves of nearby trees receive the warning that it is under attack and begin their defenses pumping anti-herbivore phenols through its system. The trees will also summon help. The airborne distress signals bring predatory insects to lay eggs and kill the herbivores damaging the leaves. Perfumed by a cloud of chemicals when insects swarm to eat their leaves, the acacia signals ants living inside the tree to mobilize in defense, especially when the environment is dry and the leaves are important to conserve water.

On the Asian continent those considering the words of Jesus know the choice is likely to bring death. It brings beatings, imprisonment, banishment, or loss of all that is familiar and secure. The warnings are all around them. The promises of grace also pass between the believers to continue their calling another day, counting it a privilege to witness to others even in prison or wash the feet of the persecutors with prayer for their souls. Children who have not seen their dad or mom because they are held in these jails or killed for their faith grow proud of the ability not to deny Christ. These are children who know that God gave us everything when he gave us Christ because the moment hovers when they will have lost everything but Christ.

In that day they will say, Surely this is our God; we trusted in him, and he saved us. This is the LORD, we trusted in him; let us rejoice and be glad in his salvation (Isa 25:9).

Iran, a part of Mesopotamia, the land between the Tigris and Euphrates rivers, was once a place where the words of Christ were received.

> Now there were staying in Jerusalem God-fearing Jews from every nation under heaven. When they heard this sound, a crowd came together in bewilderment, because each one heard their own language being spoken. Utterly amazed, they asked: Aren't all these who are speaking Galileans? Then how is it that each of us hears them in our native language?' Parthians, Medes and Elamites; residents of Mesopotamia, Judea and Cappadocia, Pontus and Asia, Phrygia and Pamphylia, Egypt and the parts of Libya near Cyrene; visitors from Rome (both Jews and converts to Judaism); Cretans and Arabs—we hear them declaring the wonders of God in our own tongues!" (Acts 2:5–11).

Two thousand years later, Saeed Abedini, a pastor, a father, and husband from Idaho, is being held in one of Iran's toughest prisons because he returned to his homeland to share the news of Christ.[6] During a visit to Tehran to see family and to finalize the board members for an orphanage he was building in Iran, Saeed was arrested by the Iranian Revolutionary Guard on July 28, 2012. He was interrogated and told to wait under house arrest for a court summons. Instead of a summons, reminiscent of the soldiers who came for Jesus, members of the Guard raided his parents' home in Tehran on September 26, 2012, confiscated Saeed's belongings and took him to an unknown location. Four days later the Guard informed the family that he was confined in solitaire in the Evin prison. For weeks Saeed, thirty-four years old, sat alone in the small cell, brought out only to be interrogated. Cut off from his wife and two young children in the US, he's been denied medical care for the infections resulting from being beaten because as a Christian he is considered an infidel.

These lands are filled with mothers who know they may never see their sons again and fathers who won't raise their daughters.

---

6. Facebook, "Pray for Pastor Saeed Abedini"

When God designed the trees to alert each other in times of stress, he also considered the hearts of his people who would be afflicted and he forged the new community that would be the body of Christ. Mary, standing quietly at the cross where her son Jesus hung dying, held the words spoken to her by the angel when she was a young girl. Jesus looked upon her and told her that John was now her son. He looked at John and told him that Mary was now his mother.

"I will not leave you as orphans," Jesus had said (John 14:8). "I will come to you."

Bringing together his people through the Holy Spirit, news of Saeed swept the world's believers into prayer. A petition quickly received media attention with more than 610,000 signatures asking for Saeed's release. On his 1,000 day in prison, June 22, 2015, evangelicals laid 1,000 flowers on the steps of the US Capital in continued prayer. His case was argued before the United Nations bringing to light the plight of the persecuted.

The trial of Jesus lasted only hours, but there was purpose in the miscarriage of justice. It was vital in how it would reach through the ages to bring us to his tree of the cross. From the moment they arrested Jesus under cover of darkness, they broke the laws of Moses that instructed this be carried out only in daylight. The Jewish legal system given to Moses and his people required them to appoint judges and officers in every town to judge with righteous judgment, without partiality, and to never take a bribe "that you may inherit the land that God is giving you." The high priest who questioned Jesus was the one who had conspired with Judas. In the early morning hours, about seventy priests, teachers of the law, and elders gathered. In Matthew 26 we are told how they were seeking false testimony against Jesus so they could put him to death. They found none. The enemy's words condemning faith in Jesus rarely brings a criticism against Jesus himself, how he was drawn to heal the leper, the child of a distraught mother, a crippled man, giving sight to a blind man, restoring Lazarus from the dead to be with his family, curing Peter's mother-in-law when she was ill, and the servant of a Roman soldier who was at death's door.

None of our persecutors speak of Jesus standing with arms outstretched, offering water to the thirsty, beckoning to come to him because he is gentle, humble of heart, willing to share our burdens. Still today unbelievers among the lost will find ways to do away with Christ so they can keep a sense of control under their own authority and not have their deceptions exposed. The trials that the mocked, imprisoned, and persecuted face today are as unfair as the trial of Jesus that violated Old Testament laws. His was conducted in private, not in public. In Jewish law capital offense trials were required to take place over two days and mandated a defense be heard. At dawn the decision was already made. Matthew 27 tells of how they bound him and delivered him for Roman trial. Pilate would see the accusations as only religious blasphemy which didn't concern the Romans, so the Jewish leaders changed the charges to sedition, a Roman crime.

Pilate concluded there was no guilt in this man. Jesus had done nothing worthy of death but the people insisted he was a threat. When Pilate learned Jesus was a Galilean who belonged to Herod's district who was in Jerusalem at the time, he sent him there. Herod was the king who had beheaded John the Baptist. He was the son of the Herod who had ordered the slaughter of infants thirty years earlier. Herod questioned Jesus but Jesus would not answer. He was sent back to Pilate.

Pilate called together the leaders and said that both he and Herod had not found Jesus guilty of any accusations. He was going to release Jesus but the shouts of the crowd prevailed. Pilate released Barabbas instead and delivered Jesus over to his death. Those who betrayed and condemned him fulfilled God's plan so they themselves could be redeemed.

Long ago you broke off your yoke and tore off your bonds; you said, "I will not serve you!" Indeed, on every high hill and under every spreading tree you lay down as a prostitute (Jer 2:20).

> You burn with lust among the oaks and under every spreading tree; you sacrifice your children in the ravines and under the overhanging crags (Isa 57:5).

God remains faithful, unmovable as a tree beckoning the birds from a raging storm, the blossoming branches providing nests for the young to continue. Come, Jesus invites, share in the tree of life. Our wandering hearts are called to return.

Two different tree of life symbols are used in Kabbalah, the Jewish tradition underlying Christianity.[7] One tree, the tree of emanation, is upside down growing out of heaven's pattern. Rooted in infinite light the branches reach down toward earth to nourish our spiritual and physical lives. The other tree of life is rooted in earth, reaching upward toward the infinite heaven, striving toward the source of all life. The roots and branches grow into the future, each new generation extending God's wisdoms.

> It is a tree of life to all who take hold of it (Prov 3:18).

> Do not let them out of your sight, keep them within your heart; for they are life to those who find them and health to one's whole body (Prov 4:22).

> This will bring health to your body and nourishment to your bones (Prov 3:8).

> They are a garland to grace your head and a chain to adorn your neck (Prov 1:9).

Alive and growing, the tree gives us shelter. Its vitality supports all in its environment with fruit, shade from the heat, and protection from the winds. We can hold on to it even as the leaves change hues and fall to the ground because through Christ we are grafted into the root system. The fruit from the tree of knowledge changed the world with fruits of despair, leaving us vulnerable to the serpent's suggestion to seek our own satisfactions instead of God's knowledge. It brought death. The tree of life bears the eternal fruit, now guarded by cherubims with a flaming sword east of the garden (Gen 3:22–24). We find it by entering Christ's words. The tree can restore righteousness and the gravity from the weight

---

7. The Kabbalah Center, "What is Kabbalah"

of our fears no longer holds us earthbound. From its crown we can see above to the infinite blessings of our Creator.

The goodness of its fruit God grows in a person's life cannot be known if we are forbidden to speak about it. When Jesus was approached and someone called him good, he said there is only one good—God. Integrity to be transparent so the light can shine through and speak openly with God derives its source from God's water of life. Reflecting God, we are to always be listening to respond to the cry of distress, cleansing within where we are made of both dark and light, selfish and generous, doubt and faith, kindness and hardness. The relief brought by Paul saying to walk in the Spirit meant God understands that we cannot do it by ourselves. It means we are known to God even when we grow faint.

David, the writer of psalms, said surely goodness and mercy shall follow all the days of his life. Both are needed, for the times of jubilee and the mercy for the times of persecution. As king, David, beloved of God, grieving over the loss of a son and guilt from having had a soldier killed, walked along with his convoy of troops and special guards. Shimei, a man from the clan of Saul who David had replaced as king, came along and cursed David. Shimei had lost everything and wanted retaliation.

> He pelted David and all the king's officials with stones, though all the troops and the special guard were on David's right and left. As he cursed, Shimei said, "Get out, get out, you murderer, you scoundrel! The Lord has repaid you for all the blood you shed in the household of Saul, in whose place you have reigned. The Lord has given the kingdom into the hands of your son Absalom. You have come to ruin because you are a murderer!" (2Sam 6:6–8).

Walking with David, Abishai, a soldier, asked to be allowed to kill him. But David said no, if God has put him there they were to endure the onslaught of words. "Leave him alone; let him curse, for the LORD has told him to," David said. "It may be that the LORD will look upon my misery and restore to me his covenant blessing instead of his curse today" (v11–12). Shimei went along the hillside opposite them, cursing as he went, throwing stones at him and showering him with dirt.

David and his people continued on to the place of rest.

David had reminded his soldier that God is still in control. He left justice with God. The disciples were told the same. Leave revenge to the righteous judgment of God. Instead, grow the fruits of the Spirit that will leave a legacy to the generations to come. The writer of Psalm 71 begins in desperation because he is surrounded by enemies who say, "God has forsaken him; pursue him and seize him, for no one will rescue him." (v 11).

Be my rock of refuge, to which I can always go; give the command to save me, for you are my rock and my fortress. Deliver me, my God, from the hand of the wicked, from the grasp of those who are evil and cruel (v3–4).

Then, as he's remembering how the Sovereign Lord has been his hope, his confidence since his youth, he declares God's righteousness in a rising crescendo.

> I will always have hope; I will praise you more and more. My mouth will tell of your righteous deeds, of your saving acts all day long though I know not how to relate them all. I will come and proclaim your mighty acts, Sovereign Lord; I will proclaim your righteous deeds, yours alone" (v 15–16).

These are the seeds the psalmist wants to leave for others. "Even when I am old and gray, do not forsake me, my God, till I declare your power to the next generation, your mighty acts to all who are to come" (v18).

The blossoming branch is beautiful. The Lord had it used to decorate the Menorah with oil cups in the shape of almond blossoms (Exod 25:33,34,37). The Hebrew word for almond is *shakeid* which comes from the root word "to watch" or "wake." The Menorah is a symbol of the Tree of Life. Christianity's trees are both the doorway that sin entered the world and the tree that was hammered into a cross for the creation to be restored to God. The righteous branch who gives life is Jesus, well rooted in God's will.

"I am like an olive tree flourishing in the house of God; I trust in God's unfailing love forever and ever" (Ps 52:8).

For twenty centuries the Lord's seeds took root and the carriers have been persecuted here where the message of this unfailing love began. Emerging in the first century, the message spread from Jerusalem throughout the near east, into Syria, Asia Minor, and Egypt. The message went out into the world, across the lands, across oceans, cultures, and political barriers. Its words are carried with worries of crossing borders, being caught, persecuted, not knowing if they'd make it home. Everywhere it went the noise of industrialization followed with loss of healthy lands where trees sustained life. Everywhere it went persecution followed like a predator hunting its prey.

Blessed are those who are invited to the wedding supper of the Lamb! (Rev 19:9).

On the evening of December 13, 2014, Bhim Nayak, pastor of Banjara Baptist Church in New Delhi and a group of fifteen from his congregation were singing Christian carols to families.[8] As their faces lifted, their voices bringing worship, they were brutally beaten with sticks and clubs wielded by about three dozen Hindus. International Christian Concern reported a twenty-eight-year-old Christian husband and his twenty-five-year-old, five month pregnant wife were locked in a factory office and beaten, dragged out into public, stoned, and then burned alive by a mob of angry Muslims in the Chak village in November 2014.[9]

Barnabas Fund reported six Hmong families in Laos who converted to Christianity on November 1, 2014 were forced out of their village after refusing to renounce their faith.[10] The families had to walk away from their homes, farms, and possessions. Earlier that month authorities arrested seven Hmong in Laos who

---

8. Church in Chains, "India: Pastor and carol singers attacked by Hindu extremists"

9. Worthy Christian News, "Pakistan: Christian Couple Burned Alive"

10. Barnabas Fund, "Lao Hmong Christian families evicted after converting to Christianity"

proclaimed faith in Jesus. The five who renounced their faith were released. The other two were sent to prison.

On October 12, 2014 Worthy News posted the story of Barry Barnett, a messianic Jew who the Ministry of the Interior deported from Israel for ten years.[11] Barry was arrested on November 20, 2013 near the city of Be'er Shiva by immigration enforcement officers at a Jews for Jesus rally called "Behold your God, Israel." He was interrogated for four days at the immigration detention before a court hearing accused him of violating the terms of his B-2 tourist visa by doing missionary work. Lawyers for Jews for Jesus in Israel lost their appeal to the lower court in March 2015 and appealed to the Supreme Court citing that as a signatory of the Global Code of Ethics for Tourism, Israel affirmed the validity of tourism for the purpose of exchanging religious beliefs. Barry will not be able to attend any appeal because of being banned.

The poor and needy search for water, but there is none; their tongues are parched with thirst. But I the LORD will answer them; I, the God of Israel, will not forsake them (Isa 41:17).

The heart of God watches as tens of thousands of missiles and rockets are poised, pointing at Israel. God responds with the promise to restore the wasteland and quench the bereaved with springs of water that bring strength.

> I will put in the desert the cedar and the acacia, the myrtle and the olive. I will set junipers in the wasteland, the fir and the cypress together, so that people may see and know, may consider and understand, that the hand of the Lord has done this that the Holy One of Israel has created it (v19–20).

Israel is a crossroads for more than 500 million birds migrating across her skies to Africa in the autumn and returning to Europe and Asia in the spring. Birds follow the stretch along the Judean and Samarian hills, the Jordan Valley or the Eilat mountains. Midway between Jerusalem and Tel Aviv researchers have been coming together from Europe, where the birds nest,

---

11. DeCaro, "Deported Messianic Jew to Appeal Supreme Court"

the Middle East where the birds fly through, and Africa where the birds winter. They convene at the International Center for the Study of Bird Migration that participates with more than 200 schools throughout the world in a project called Migrating Birds Know No Boundaries. The Internet project weaves regional cooperation among the peoples as it combines science of bird migration with concerns of travel.

Species facing extinction are acute in Israel because of population growth tapping natural resources and open spaces. Hundreds of nature reserves protect the trees, the last stronghold for many of the wildlife, but may overlap military training areas or habitat may be fragmented by development. Gazelles, wolves, leopards, and bats cannot thrive in these small areas.

Protecting Israel's land for future generations is requiring man and earth to work together for God's plan. As the ailing birds and trees bring people in shared concern, Jews and Christians are banding together for the first time in modern history to protect Christians in the Middle East. The World Jewish Congress, the International Christian Embassy and Empowered21 have come together like a stand of strong trees.[12]

"Some 120,000 were killed last year and no one says anything. Everyone's focusing on Gaza now and the fact is the world is coming apart," said World Jewish Congress President Rom Lauder at the annual Feast of Tabernacles celebration in Jerusalem. On October 19, 2014 the Christian Broadcasting Network reported that Rom, an advocate for Jews around the world, encouraged more than 4,000 Christians from eighty nations attending the Feast of Tabernacles to work together as one to be strengthened. Citing Paul's second letter to Timothy, he reminded that God did not give us a spirit of fear but the spirit of power.

By the early twentieth century Israel's indigenous forests had been nearly destroyed. In 1948 when Israel was established there were fewer than 5 million trees standing. The cedar of Lebanon was under threat from generations of logging, goat grazing, and

---

12. Stahl and Mitchell, "Christians, Jews Team Up to Fight Against Islamic Persecution"

ASIA

developing resorts and tourism. The once huge trees foresting the land are now in small fragmented patches. Young trees already struggling against insect infestation and disease also face a changing climate that could warm the mountainous areas and leave the cedars with nowhere to grow.

Now God is restoring the land. The Hebrew language is also being restored, calling upon the name of Yeshua in Hebrew prayers once again throughout the land. Israel again is blossoming from the desolation of deforestations.

I will give them a new heart to know me, the Lord says (Ezek 36:26).

More than 200 million native trees have been planted to reforest the land of Israel. Initiated by the Jewish National Fund, early plantings of evergreens in the mountainous regions and eucalyptus in the south extended to restore trees such as oaks, carobs, terebinths, cypress, olive, and almond trees.[13] Reminding how God cherishes the scent of cedar filling his temple, gentle hands prepare soil in sunlit places for the roots to grow deep, tap down the soil around it and soak the ground with water.

> All the birds of the sky nested in its boughs, all the animals of the wild gave birth under its branches; all the great nations lived in its shade. It was majestic in beauty, with its spreading boughs, for its roots went down to abundant waters. The cedars in the garden of God could not rival it, nor could the junipers equal its boughs, nor could the plane trees compare with its branches—no tree in the garden of God could match its beauty (Ezek 31:3–8).

> But the tree was brought down to the realm of the dead and covered the deep springs with mourning. The sound of its falling down to the pit made nations tremble. God then restrained the abundant waters. "Because of it I clothed Lebanon with gloom, and all the trees of the field withered away. Then all the trees of Eden, the choicest

13. Jewish National Fund, "Plant Trees in Israel"

and best of Lebanon, the well-watered trees, were consoled in the earth below. They too, like the great cedar, had gone down to the realm of the dead, to those killed by the sword, along with the armed men who lived in its shade among the nations, (v15–17).

"This is Pharaoh and all his hordes," declares the Sovereign Lord (v18). The splendor had perished. God brings down the powerful and proud.

The cedar's beauty on the hills of Lebanon give an aromatic scent of balsam in the sap of its bark and cones, so fragrant in the forest that in Hosea 14 as the Lord calls the people to turn back to him, he says "like a cedar of Lebanon he will send down his roots; his young shoots will grow. His fragrance will be like a cedar of Lebanon." The tall cedars of Lebanon constructed Solomon's palace and were chosen for the temple to display God's glory in Jerusalem.

He lined its interior walls with cedar boards, paneling them from the floor of the temple to the ceiling, and covered the floor of the temple with planks of juniper (1 Kgs 6:15).

The inside of the temple was cedar, carved with gourds and open flowers. Everything was cedar; no stone was to be seen (1 Kgs 6:18).

He covered the altar with cedar (1 Kgs 6:20).

He built the Palace of the Forest of Lebanon a hundred cubits long, fifty wide and thirty high, with four rows of cedar columns supporting trimmed cedar beams (1 Kgs 7:2).

He built the throne hall, the Hall of Justice, where he was to judge, and he covered it with cedar from floor to ceiling (1 Kgs 7:7).

The cedar tree flowers in May. Found in the Hermon, the Galilee and the Judean mountains, its oils and timber have aided humans for thousands of years, building ships, and being used for burials. The cedar grows slowly, maturing into fissured bark around a wide girth, able to survive more than a thousand years, its slender needles bluish-green growing high above the ground in tufts and spirals on wide reaching branches, often not reproducing until forty-years-old.

As his life stood among enemies mocking him, the psalmist thought of his roots deep beneath earth where God's abundant water sustained him. "Who is like you, God? Though you have made me see troubles, many and bitter, you will restore my life again; from the depths of the earth you will again bring me up. You will increase my honor and comfort me once more" (Ps 71:19–21).

6

AUSTRALIA

―――――

Let a little water be brought, and then you may all wash your feet and rest under this tree. (Gen 18:4)

Touching the intricate designs carved in the smooth bark of a tree hundreds of years ago, people on the Sunshine Coast of Australia become aware of the cherished history of those here before them. The ancient symbols, called dendroglyphs, were made by someone who once stood here with their clan to talk of births and deaths or resources and weather. When the stone ax was used to etch the pieces of bark from the side of the tree, the people were careful not to harm sapwood that moves water up to the leaves. Ashes used for healing their own wounds were applied to the exposed wood. The trees were treasured. They would be needed for shelter, canoes, and sustaining nature's ecosystem.

A tree near Nambour features a figure thought to depict a creation spirit from the Dreamtime, a long ago time when earth was being created. Another near the Mooloola River three centuries old may mark a path or a boundary. Box and red gum eucalupt trees have ceremonial rectangular and diamond rings where a council may have gathered. All over the southeast of the continent, along rivers, around lakes and on flood plains where the Koori people lived, the trees link the 23 million people living here today with the people of the last millennia.

The smallest continent, Australia's 2.9 million square miles is one country. There are plants and animals living only here in climates of tropical, desert and grasslands, now dry and thirsty from changes in the winds from the Antarctic. The continent is swept by storms. The sky over Sydney buried the city in an enormous hailstorm in April 2015. In February 2011 Cyclone Yasi crossed the western coast blasting winds 180 mph, pushing down homes, tearing roofs off buildings, and destroying power lines. Lifting waves as high as 39 feet, the cyclone surrounded people with floods, cutting off water supplies, and trapping them from reach. Surrounded by sea, Australia is least influenced by invasive species disrupting nature. But the plight of hostility toward being a Christian has found its way.

In the late 1860s many Muslims began traveling to Australia with others who wanted to explore and develop the outback. Among them, Bashda Mahommed Gool and Mullah Abdullah from Pakistan settled to live peaceably in New South Wales on the east coast, until New Year's Day 1915.[1] That day 1,200 picnickers on forty open ore trucks were traveling from Broken Hill for the annual gathering in Silverton. The two Muslim men lay in wait for them with rifles, opening fire on the convoy, killing four, and wounding seven before being killed by police.

Gool Mahomed had a note tucked into his belt that said, "I must kill you and give my life for my faith, Allāhu Akbar." Mullah Abdullah's letter said he was dying in obedience to the order of the Sultan. The two acted as individual jihads.

A century later in December 2014 the Gatestone Institute reported strangers in a car flying the Islamic State flag shouted at members of Our Lady of Lebanon Church on the west side of Sydney with threats to "kill the Christians" and "slaughter their

---

1. Durie, "One Hundred Years of Jihad in Australia"

children."[2] The flag carried the message, "There is only one god and Muhammad is the prophet." Police were dispatched to patrol the area during mass.

The following year BBC reported young women being recruited by the IS through social media and trying to leave Melbourne to join the IS fight in the Middle East.[3] Two were unaccounted for and four made it to Turkey before being turned back by authorities. A Task Force formed in April 2015 to monitor Victorians thought to be involved with IS. Two forensic psychiatrists are on the Task Force trying to understand why youth are lured. Being sold a romantic view of life, they encounter sexual servitude and arranged marriages. More than a hundred Australians were found to be supporting militant groups in the Middle East.

Moses warned his people about turning a deaf mind to God's words. "Your sons and daughters will be given to another nation, and you will wear out your eyes watching for them day after day, powerless to lift a hand." "You will have sons and daughters but you will not keep them, because they will go into captivity." (Deut 28:32,41).

In 2011, 70 percent of all marriages were performed by civil celebrants, rather than in a church. Among reasons suggested by the source, ABS Census of Population and Housing 1971- 2011, was that despite the trend moving away from formal religion, people want rituals to mark life events.[4]

The ABS Census reported the number of people stating they have no religion has been drastically increasing in Australia during the past century, from one in 250 people to one in every five in 2011. In 1911 there were 10,000 people, 0.4 percent of the population, who chose the option "no religion" on their Census form. In 2011 there were nearly 4.8 million, 22 percent of the population, who had no belief in God.

The number of people who reported being an atheist almost doubled from 31,300 in 2006 to 58,900 people in 2011. The survey

---

2. Ibrahim, "Christians and Churches Attacked in the West"
3. BBC News, "Young Australian women trying to join IS"
4. Australia Bureau of Statistics, "Australian Social Trends"

cites the Atheist Foundation of Australia led a campaign to report no religion on the Census. The campaign was also carried out in New Zealand and the United Kingdom. New Zealand's Census showed a rise from 30 percent in 2001 to 35 percent in 2006. Rates in England and Wales went from 15 percent in 2001 to 25 percent in 2011. Canadian rates rose from 16 percent to 24 percent during these years. In the United States the General Social Survey showed the rate of American adults reporting no religion to be 20 percent in 2012 compared with 14 percent in 2000. The 2011 Census in Ireland showed those who report no religion are now the second largest grouping in the country behind Catholics, with the number increasing more than four-fold since 1991.

The highest numbers among those reporting no faith are youth under thirty years old. Only 10 percent of the population in Australia aged sixty-five and older reported no religion in 2011.

A worldview without Jesus is expanding through the young following the world like the tail of a comet. They are not hearing Jesus say, "Come to me, find rest for your souls." The young are struggling without the tool Jesus has given us—his yoke. It is an easy yoke, Jesus said, fit perfectly to each individual, measured to balance the weight we carry when we share in the work God is doing. Paul clarifies this saying, "Do not be yoked together with unbelievers. For what do righteousness and wickedness have in common? Or what fellowship can light have with darkness?" (2Cor 6:14). In Deut. 22:10 the Israelites were instructed not to yoke a donkey and an ox together to plow the soil. They do not have the same gait, the same nature, or the same life choices. The soil will not be prepared well.

Youth contending with the world turning up the volume of its messages will not take root as the deceiver floods media through their every sense, the sights and sounds into their minds. Soil plowed and overturned to bring to the surface how Jesus was rejected, how he understood the loneliness of a prophet's life because he was different, teaches the unique commonality believers face if they choose the path of life. Dishonored and scorned, messengers of the Word find their safeness is in the sanctuary of God where "splendor and majesty are before him; strength and joy are in his dwelling place" (1Chr 16:27).

The words cultivated in the furrows of soil bring God's people around youth with words that echo the voice of rushing waters, the sound of many thunders that resound with the chorus of hallelujahs in heaven, and the land becomes radiant with his glory. The elders bring the light of the sun and weed out the doubts that loneliness in this world can bring. We are to be a hedge around the newly growing seeds in the way we stand.

Jesus took on the concerns of sinners and showed how they could grow roots to thrive on living waters that will never leave them thirsty. They could revive the dry branches that were brittle and breaking. They could adorn their lives with leaves fresh and green in a new morning's sun and fruit that would bring seeds for others to grow.

But they must be the seeds of God and not the presence of invasive shoots that can choke a tender growth. The University of Melbourne found young alpine and mountain ash woodlands are dying in parts of Victoria, Tasmania, and the Snowy Mountains. Fostered by climate change, bushfires are erupting more often and young trees are less able to regenerate, burnt before they can produce seeds.

Logging along with the pollution it causes brought more change and the invasive ash, called wattle trees, took over the spaces.

Wattles have become a globally invasive problem, taking over grasslands and spread by mild climates. The Australian and New Zealand Weed Risk Assessment gives it a high risk score of fifteen as one of the world's top hundred most invasive species.[5] The entire creation is groaning under afflictions, feeling the choking loneliness, waiting for the return of Jesus. Temperatures in Australia have risen 33 degrees F in the past century. In 1880 the sea level was 8.27 inches lower than in 2011. The surface of the sea around the coast is nearly 30 degrees warmer than it was in 1910. Scientists say it's due to carbon dioxide concentrating in the atmosphere

---

5. Werren, "Environmental Weeds of the Wet Tropics"

from fossil fuel combustion since the industrial age. The continent is projected to be 40 F degrees hotter by 2070.

> Dear friends, do not be surprised at the fiery ordeal that has come on you to test you, as though something strange were happening to you. But rejoice inasmuch as you participate in the sufferings of Christ, so that you may be overjoyed when his glory is revealed. If you are insulted because of the name of Christ, you are blessed, for the Spirit of glory and of God rests on you (1 Pet 4:12–14).

For if they do these things when the tree is green, what will happen when it is dry? (Luke 23:31).

The plumes of scented aldehydes, ketones, and esters that trees release signal danger to others who are rooted in the waters, intent on fulfilling God's design for their growth. The communication is instant throughout the community, never failing to warn or the others could fall victim.

For we are to God the pleasing aroma of Christ among those who are being saved and those who are perishing (2Cor 22:15).

The rates of reporting no religion begin rising after the age of fifteen, reaching their height between the ages of twenty-two and twenty-four.[6] The number of twenty to twenty-four year olds living on the Australian continent with no faith in God in 2011 was nearly eleven percent higher than the same individuals had reported when they were of fifteen to nineteen years old in 2006.

The ancient trees marked by the ancestors stand in quiet witness, unmovable, unchanging in their purpose. Elders hold the knowledge of God but its translation into the coming generations is being disrupted. For youth without knowledge of being rooted in Christ, trees seem to be falling around them and replaced by different species. Their world quakes with uncertainty.

To you, LORD, I call, for fire has devoured the pastures in the wilderness and flames have burned up all the trees of the field (Joel 1 1:19).

---

6. Australian Census of Population and Housing

Our Trees of Life

Ninety-six animal species on the continent have become critically endangered, the highest threat level that is assigned. A bush tailed rat kangaroo who occupies southwestern Australia is facing extinction. The tiny mountain possum and long-eared bats are all vanishing. Only about 200 wombats are holding onto an uncertain future. Potoroo marsupials and little dunnarts who can thrive only in certain habitat are disappearing.

Dust from mining has destroyed nesting sites for the Christmas Island frigatebird. The orange-bellied parrot is expected to disappear forever. The Pacific Ocean is becoming empty of the leatherback turtles. The presence of the hawksbill turtle is disappearing too along their region of the northern Australia coast. Several species of frogs on mountaintops, in swamps, in streams and creeks, bogs, and forests are being pushed out of existence.

In the waters the fish are threatened because of invasive species and overfishing. The spotted handfish, a fish that walks on its fins across the sea bed in southeast Tasmania, harrison's dogfish in the deep waters off the eastern coast, the goby from artesian springs in western Queensland, northern river sharks, bluefin tuna, are all critical species. Urban expansion in southern Sydney is extinguishing a dragonfly called the Sydney hawk. Famous in Australia, the stick insect is now bred in captivity in an effort to return its numbers to creation. Four species of katydids, along with crustacians and mollusks are needing help.

In 2012 the Australian federal government listed the giant kelp forests near Tasmania, Victoria, and southern Australia as an endangered community.[7] Kelp are seaweeds growing into seabed forests waving graceful leaves to protect underwater species. Sea urchins, blackfish, groupers, abalone, and little worms swim among these forests. Nurseries of fishes are nested here. Divers come to admire their beauty. Companies come and build economy from their use in personal care products and in fertilizers.

The marine forests have been struggling against invasive species, pollution, and human disruptions on coastlines combining with warming oceans. Kelp may shift slowly southward into

---

7. The ABC, "Giant kelp forests granted endangered status"

deeper cooler waters but that may limit photosynthesis. Events of sudden warming could deforest an entire area, leaving bare rock, and hinder choices to further new growth elsewhere.

This is the world youth are experiencing. Their minds shattered, their hearts torn apart, the only wholeness in sight is the promise of Jesus shared when someone tells them their worth to God. The importance of choice comes from understanding the stresses on faith and managing collectively to preserve the beautiful habitat that shelters others in its song. "The righteous man grows like a cedar" (Ps 92:12). Evergreen and fragrant, God uses the cedar's many gifts to represent the ways of a Christian.

The tree towered majestically (Ezek 31:3). Its mighty branches shade the mountains (Ps 80:10).The young shoots will grow and bring fragrance (Hos 14:6). Its strength will hold up the temple (1Kings 6:9). The wood is dependable enough to be chosen for a mast (Ezek 27:5). Through all seasons of heat and cold, the cedar endures, evergreen, seeking God continually while working its ministry (2Tim 4:5).

Cedar was used with hyssop to cleanse from disease (Lev 14:4). We are to continually cleanse each other from the dust of the world. God planted the tree to bring moisture. "The trees of the Lord are well watered, the cedars of Lebanon that he planted" (Ps 104:16). Being well watered preserves God's words to stay fresh and green even in old age (Ps 92). The cedar's oil was used to preserve parchment and the wood kept moths away from eating holes in garments and blankets.

Their growth is assured. "Like valleys they spread out, like gardens beside a river, like aloes planted by the Lord, like cedars beside the waters" (Num 24:6). They are our protection. Jeremiah warned his country they had strayed from God. In response, they threw him in a pit and continued to follow their own plans. After forty years of warnings, God said, "I will send destroyers against you, each man with his weapons, and they will cut up your fine cedar beams and throw them into the fire" (Jer 22:7).

The red cedar growing throughout Australia south to the basaltic soils, west to the village of Termeil is among the few native deciduous trees on the continent. The red timber is highly valued for furniture, panelling, and ship building. Exploited in the nineteenth and early twentieth centuries, nearly all the old trees were cut down. The cedar became less available and its gifts were no longer abundant.

The word of the Lord prevails because each part of the tree is designed to work together in continuing the fruit's presence in their graceful offspring. The crown of branches and leaves brings in light for photosynthesis that makes the energy for the tree. The roots anchor the tree to bring in water and nutrients for the entire tree. The trunk rises from the roots to support the crown of leaves. In it the sapwood carries water and nutrients up from the roots, through the branches to the leaves, and distributes the sap that the leaves and needles make.

Sapwood is created by the tree's cambium cells that create continued growth in the trunk by making a new layer of sapwood and a new layer of bark each year. Heartwood forms when sapwood completes its job and is replaced by new sapwood. The heartwood gives the tree its strength to stand. It is not a living, changeable fluid tissue but solidly made, unchanging. The outer bark encases the tree to hold in moisture and shield the tree from damage, disease, and the changes of heat and cold. Leaves on the outer crown high above are on the front line with the sun absorbing more photosynthesis than the leaves beneath them shaded.

"We are hard pressed on every side, but not crushed; perplexed, but not in despair; persecuted, but not abandoned; struck down, but not destroyed," Paul wrote. The lonely man of God collided with the world's thinking in every court of his day. As one chosen to be on the front lines to insure heartwood would be strong, he said, "We always carry around in our body the death of Jesus, so that the life of Jesus may also be revealed in our body. For we who are alive are always being given over to death for Jesus' sake, so that his life may also be revealed in our mortal body" (2Cor 4:8–11).

> On the mountain heights of Israel I will plant it; it will produce branches and bear fruit and become a splendid

cedar. Birds of every kind will nest in it; they will find shelter in the shade of its branches (Ezek 17:23).

The fruit of the Spirit is faithfulness and it is gentle (Gal 5:22–23).

Responsive to the Spirit, gentleness advances communion with God. Jesus said, "Learn from me for I am gentle" (Matt 11:29). Yet this gentleness of a God who humbled himself for our sake is attacked, reviled, and chased down like a bird to be caught in a net.

Matthew's first thought of Jesus' death is in chapter 16 when Jesus begins to tell his disciples that he must die. He must go to Jerusalem and suffer at the hands of the elders, the priests, and the teachers of the law. He's preparing them to understand that not only will he suffer, but they also will suffer and the heartwood will be renewed. The seeds will multiply. Then Jesus said to his disciples, "Whoever wants to be my disciple must deny themselves and take up their cross and follow me. For whoever wants to save their life will lose it, but whoever loses their life for me will find it" (v 24–25). He speaks to those who would later see his agony in the garden of Gethsemane so they will know he will be raised on the third day. He will return to them. "For the Son of Man is going to come in his Father's glory with his angels, and then he will reward each person according to what they have done" (v26).

He unveiled what is to come to these select few who had gone away to a high mountain to witness the Lord transfigured in the essence of his true glorious light. To prepare them to withstand his death and their own persecution, God gave them a glimpse of the astounding glory that leads believers, heals wounds, emboldens voices, and faithfully seeks the victims of the world with the Spirit's gentleness.

The fragrance dwelling in the shelter of the Most High brings memory of a promised home.

Distinctive Australian style paintings express eucalyptus in the landscapes, a symbol of the unique scented oil rising from the bush in a blue haze that gave the Blue Mountains their name. From tall trees to small shrubs, the eucalupts grow everywhere except the high alpine regions. They stand to serve shelter for many of

Australia's animals and birds. Koalas thrive on the gum leaves. Eucalypts have given generations of the aboriginal people tools, shields, dishes, canoes, medicines, food, and musical instruments. As timber their unique grain patterns provide for Australian artwork.

Many of these trees have seeds encased by woody capsules to protect against fire. The heat of fire will release their seeds to regenerate new trees. They are beneficial to other trees, lowering the water table to prevent flooding, providing wind breaks, and shade as one of God's community.

The trees mark Australia's history.

The first explorers to travel the continent from south to north, Burke and Wills, stopped in Queenland in December 1860, where they split into two parties. Before Burke embarked on a 400 mile journey to Melbourne he buried a cache of provisions under a tree on Cooper's Creek in Thargomindah. Today the Burke and Wills Dig Tree is an Australian national icon under the trusteeship of the Royal Historical Society of Queensland.

The tree of knowledge in Barcaldine, Queensland was the meeting place during a strike in 1891 when unions forged a connection to become the Australian Labor Party. The tree has been memorialized as the place where the party was founded.

Trees are monuments to the truths we leave for future generations. "And Joshua recorded these things in the Book of the Law of God. Then he took a large stone and set it up there under the oak near the holy place of the LORD" (Josh 24:26). The roots of these teachers have gone before us to show us where the wealth of water can be found.

Listen to advice and accept discipline, and at the end you will be counted among the wise (Prov 19:20).

Now then, my sons, listen to me; do not turn aside from what I say (Prov 5:7).

In a deafening conflicted world, who will hold reverence for the Lord "that tremble at the commandment of our God" (Ezra 10:3), unafraid to be like a cedar and hold up rafters over the young where they may take root in the foundation. The crowd that turned against Jesus was disappointed because he didn't fulfill their expectations of what they wanted for themselves. Do we dare let the coming generation make the same mistake? Some do not have knowledge of God, Paul wrote (1Cor 15:34). "I say this to your shame," he said. The prophet Hosea declared a country exchanges its glory for shame when it ignores God's words. His sobering words warn, "Because you have ignored the law of your God, I will ignore your children." (Hos 4:6). Setting focus on all the words God gives us roots us in waters of life, "that it may go well with you and with your children after you, and that you may live long in the land" (Deut 4:40), because by his words, God has given us life (Ps 119:93).

The tender shoots growing from earth turning their faces upward in quiet trust for the morning sun, bending their growth to its warm shining rays, wanting to unfold their gifts, are vulnerable to the heavy footsteps that crush them down. Words sung by the elders can move our faint spirit into strength with God assuring, "You did not choose me, but I chose you and appointed you so that you might go and bear fruit—fruit that will last" (John 15:16).

The disciples have watered us with prayer, "May the God of hope fill you with all joy and peace as you trust in him, so that you may overflow with hope by the power of the Holy Spirit" (Rom 15:13). We are to take this abundant water and continue to prepare the soil to transform seeds into new trees bearing fruit.

Christianity arrived in Australia on the First Fleet in May 1787 when Britain sent eleven ships of more than a thousand convicts and seamen along with supplies to found the first European settlement. During the next centuries Buddhist, Confucian, Hindu, Islamic, Taoist, and other practices arrived. In 1901 the Australian constitution provided for freedom of religion.

The music of the land has taken on hymns in every style from a choral evensong to country music. People gather in the open air for Christmas carols in Melbourne and Sydney with the Christmas story taking place in the warm red dust of Australia. Easter traditions brought by migrant communities, Greek Orthodox, and fishermen from Sicily are shared on the land to bring a diversity of sounds.

Emerging is a succession of faith without the fragmentation of people in the way trees can be separated into single groves and not support as much life. A forest of divergent gifts developing from bare soil to mature trees proceeds steadily over time from herbaceous plants to woody shrubs to pioneer trees that require full sun, then trees that will grow in their shade. The growth can be influenced by wildfire, wind, lightning, flood, drought, bugs, disease, and human interference but they will continue, intent on filling the land. Each member grows to bring about its part of a forest that creates an edge effect between communities.

Edge effects in the diversity of people is a transition place between two different ecotones, mirroring a gradual mixing at the edge of the forest where plants and many types of trees grow, more gifted together than either is alone. The woods edge supports species not found in either the clearing or the deep woods but in the transition space.

Australia's spirituality today is infused with the people of the eucaluptus, the kelp forests, and the dry earth places. Indigenous peoples have customs for mourning and celebrations for births. In the seventeenth century Portuguese, Spanish Catholics, Dutch, and English Protestants sailed the Australian waters, bringing a permanent presence of the Bible. By the nineteenth century immigrants came from a range of church denominations each with an expression of Christianity as they founded churches on the southern continent in the Barossa Valley, Queensland, Sevehill, Victory, and on the northern territories.

Missions built schools among the aboriginal people as Europeans took control over more of the continent. British invasion held aboriginal lands as empty and belonging to no one before they arrived. Today there are about 500 different aboriginal groups, each with their own language and songs. The people moved seasonally throughout the year, along the coast, and at river headwaters. In the bush and desert they gathered and hunted, dependant on the types of trees both for themselves and the animals the trees drew for game.

The aboriginal people received apologies at the beginning of the twenty-first century from churches and church organizations for the injustice of being dispossessed of their land. Much of the land has been returned to them but the devastating impact it had on their communities and children continues to need healing.

The missions had also recorded linguistic and cultural aspects of the aboriginal people which have been invaluable in understanding their forebears. Traditions such as the smoking ceremonies and speaking prayers in original language are now promoted alongside the English speakers. The voices of youth are invited to join, be who they are and come give thanks. The Coming of Light Festival continues to mark the arrival of Christian missionaries to the Torres Strait Islands on July 1, 1871.

Other dwellers of the forest prefer the deep woods. The place at the edge is stressful for species who don't benefit from edge effects. Some birds and animals need undisturbed mature forest and congregate only here, building nests where there are fewer predators. Areas within the woods with crops of rocks, logs, or spring ponds can harbor endangered species and manage temperature, moisture, and light coming through the canopy. Sandy soils support pine trees. Wet soil supports cedar. The land becomes a living interdependent community growing under disturbances and changes in the weather the sky invests in our earth.

Who are we without our wounds? Wanting the days before the storm when the sky was serene, we find the answer in who God redeems us to be because of our wounds. Christians are coming together into stands of the redeemed at the news of persecutions and falling faith. Changing, adapting, always with an ordered plan, nature binds into firmaments, growing together on similar soil under shared conditions.

Australia is a country where victims of human trafficking are brought by crime groups operating out of Asia, Eastern Europe, China, Korea, and Thailand. Migrants of all ages from India, China, and South Korea who are deceived into thinking they come to work in Australia are coerced into prostitution or slave wages. They are held in bondage of debt having to work off the cost to get their passport returned to them. The Australian NGO Project Respect reports reasons for trafficking women into Australia is because of the lack of prostitutes in Australia, customer demand bringing money to crime groups, or customers who want women they can treat violently without repercussion.[8] Government workers established aid for these victims, their families, and witnesses in the prosecutions with shelter, counseling, or temporary visas. The focus is on prevention as well as encouragement for communities to speak out in uncompromising witness and be aware that we are now a global community. Australia, Cambodia, Burma, Laos, and Thailand have bonded in a coordinated anti-trafficking agreement.

Near the estuary of the Yarra River where once artisanal fishermen brought in the day's catch on open shorelines and clans of the Kulin nation gathered, today the city of Melbourne is home to more than 4 million people. On April 4, 2015, more than 3,000 gathered in Melbourne where hundreds of police formed barricades to separate the flaming tempers. Reclaim Australia members protested against the rise of Islamic extremism and sharia law in the country clashing with anti-racist groups who saw this as targeting a culture. The crowd also drew Muslims who don't accept extreme actions of their religion and wanted to bring understanding that Islam extremists do not portray their beliefs.

There are relationships among the trees with others of its species, colonizing in nature. People who settled in remote areas of Australia were less likely to report having no religion, 19 percent compared to 22 percent on average. There is rediscovered faith when relationship comes together with shared words. The presence of Wollemi pine found in a gorge near Sydney was thought to have been extinct in 1994. There are fewer than a hundred of the pines growing in the wild, threatened now by tourists, disturbed, and exposed to its seeds being trampled.

Each tree with its animals and birds has a space they need whether a wolf needing its range or a field mouse needing its safe

---

8. Humantrafficking.org, "Report on Trafficking in Australia"

routes. Breeding seasons require many types of trees and plants and winter brings need of a citadel. Interaction between species brings mutual benefit to both.

> If the root is holy, so are the branches. If some of the branches have been broken off, and you, though a wild olive shoot, have been grafted in among the others and now share in the nourishing sap from the olive root, do not consider yourself to be superior to those other branches. If you do, consider this: You do not support the root, but the root supports you. You will say then, "Branches were broken off so that I could be grafted in." Granted. But they were broken off because of unbelief, and you stand by faith. Do not be arrogant, but tremble. For if God did not spare the natural branches, he will not spare you either (Rom 11:16–21).

Paul says to stay on task communicating the truth in speaking, in music, in actions. Seasoned through the battles, stoned, beaten, rejected, imprisoned, Paul also experienced being held in esteem as he passed on his hard gained experience to Timothy. In weakness and fear as well as rejoicing and power, he prevailed because there are so many without the defense of faith who have no one else to protect them from the enemy tearing them down. Paul told Timothy that foremost be a man of prayer, continually a vessel for the living waters, and to pray for all men because we have one God.

On his way to Jerusalem, Jesus came down the road to the Mount of Olives with a crowd of disciples who were joyfully praising God. But the Pharisees told Jesus to silence his disciples. "I tell you," he replied, "If they keep quiet, the stones will cry out" (Luke 18:40).

Churches burn, believers pass to heaven, but his light multiplies across the earth because Christians believe they have a message of inestimable value for those they see are perishing.

Blessed is the one who keeps the words of the prophecy written in this scroll (Rev 22:7).

Our Trees of Life

The lost youth will know their gifts, coming to be grafted in to the faith rooted in the water of life, when the promises are told of in the home, in their community, in a church, freely spoken, freely heard. The Torah indicates this requires a determined structure.

When the tabernacle was built, acacia wood was used as its framework (Exod 37–38). The acacia grows more than 1,300 species here and around warm regions in Europe, Africa, southern Asia, and the Americas. In Australia with no mountain ranges or rivers to prevent their spread, the acacias grew all over the continent to create forests with other trees such as cypress pines. Its small five-petal flower arranges in yellow or white clusters, sometimes bringing purple or red. The seeds have been used in soups and paints. Astringents procured from boiling down the wood is high in tannins. Industry uses the acacia as a fragrance continuing its centuries long use as a perfume. Some species are valued as wood used for ornaments and highly polished furniture.

Someone had to see the gifts a young tree would bring and nurture its hope by abiding by God's instructions. They could see the promise even through the cyclones and hailstorms. The apostle John saw the door open to heaven to be shown the power and majesty of the throne in heaven and who sat there. He wept when he was shown the scrolls. Was no one worthy to bring justice to his friends who had been stoned to death, imprisoned, and executed? Who would stop the slaughter of the trees and water that sustained all life? Every focus remains on the glory of the one who saves as John is given "the revelation from Jesus Christ, which God gave him to show his servants what must soon take place" (Rev 1:1).

> And the one who sat there had the appearance of jasper and ruby. A rainbow that shone like an emerald encircled the throne. Surrounding the throne were twenty-four other thrones, and seated on them were twenty-four elders. They were dressed in white and had crowns of gold on their heads. From the throne came flashes of lightning, rumblings and peals of thunder. In front of the throne, seven lamps were blazing. These are the seven spirits of God. Also in front of the throne there was what looked like a sea of glass, clear as crystal" (Rev 4:3–6).

John describes the four living creatures like a lion, an ox, a man, and a flying eagle singing holy, holy, holy is the Lord God Almighty who was, and is, and is to come. Day and night they never stop giving glory and honor and thanks to him who sits on the throne and lives forever and ever. Twenty-four elders lay their crowns before the throne saying, "You are worthy, our Lord and God, to receive glory and honor and power, for you created all things, and by your will they were created and have their being" (v. 11).

John is beckoned to "come up here, and I will show you what must take place." As he listens he is pulled into worship aware the throne room is alive with hailing the Lord's salvation. Before he is shown the horrific drama that will unfold in the future, John beholds the promise.

> To him who loves us and has freed us from our sins by his blood, and has made us to be a kingdom and priests to serve his God and Father—to him be glory and power forever and ever! Amen. Look, he is coming with the clouds, and every eye will see him, even those who pierced him; and all peoples on earth will mourn because of him. So shall it be! Amen" (v 6,7).

He is being told that the storms will come, the trees will see struggle, but hold to this promise because despite the movement for atheism or the claims that God cannot be found in this faith, inside every seed that is sown is the heart of a newborn life.

Blessed are those who listen to me, watching daily at my doors, waiting at my doorway (Prov 8:34).

"Do not listen to what the prophets are prophesying to you; they fill you with false hopes. They speak visions from their own minds, not from the mouth of the LORD (Jer 23:16).

7

ANTARCTICA

Strengthen what remains and is about to die, for I have found your deeds unfinished in the sight of my God. (Rev 3:2)

The barrage of gunfire ends, the flames blazing a church die down, arguments in courtrooms fall to their stunned defeat, and the deafening cry of children in blood-soaked regions quiets. Silence falls, impenetrable in its grief, unhearing in mystified shock as the last light among them departs.

It's the coldest of all places of the human soul. Uncharted by most of us, the penetrating loneliness is as endless as Antarctica's barren land offering no provision or comfort.

How long, Lord, must I call for help, but you do not listen? Or cry out to you, "Violence!" but you do not save? (Hab 1:2)

At the southern extreme of our planet the sun drops beyond the icy sea in March. Splashing brilliant orange and deep purples on the frigid ocean waves, darkness spreads across the glaciers a little more each day. Winds gust at unstoppable strength expanding ice to more than double its summer size. The fifth largest of all earth's continents, the south pole holds 70 percent of the world's fresh water compressed into frozen sheets some eighteen feet thick.

A company of humpback whales swim away with a fleet of petrals in the air above migrating north for warmer waters. The male emperor penguins stay to keep eggs warm between their feet through one long winter night. The weddell seals stay too, diving beneath the ice, breaking holes with their teeth so they can breathe.

There are no countries here. No borders. An international treaty of forty-six countries governs the Antarctica. It's a fortress of cold, falling below zero to minus 100 F, a wonderland of ice that sees few visitors.

Whipping winds haunt the currents where the Atlantic, Indian, and Pacific oceans become the Southern Ocean surrounding the continent, moving easterly with impacts from people who have never seen these beaches. Climate change, ozone depletion, lead particles from gasoline combustion are carried here from South America, Australia, and New Zealand. Residue from pesticides is found in seabirds and penguins. Multiplying piles of plastic and rubbish wash onto the shores. The sky has absolute reign, governing what can be done and when as earth tilts away from the sun and the Antarctica plunges into darkness. How is it following Jesus has led us to such a place. What kind of love is this?

Yet it is here in this barren space we find that we've never had a defense on our own without the mighty oaks, the fragrant pines, rainforests towering with moisture, and growth in desert places. This is about knowing ourselves in God's glory.

As nightfall spreads into the world silencing the words of Christ almost three-quarters of the world's nations report Christians being targeted with discrimination. In 2014 the US Center for the Study of Global Christianity estimated that 100,000 Christians die each year because of their faith.[1] Open Doors estimates 322 Christians are killed every month, 214 churches and properties are destroyed, and more than 772 acts of violence are directed against believers of Christ.[2]

1. Alexander, "Are there really 100,000 new Christian martyrs every year"
2. Farbishel, "Christian Persecution: Of Whom the World is Not Worthy"

Our Trees of Life

The trees exalting God are falling.

Paul wrote to the Corinthians, "Be on your guard; stand firm in the faith; be courageous; be strong" (1Cor 16:13). Be watchful. The long night has begun.

They will seize you and persecute you, Jesus said. "They will hand you over to synagogues and put you in prison, and you will be brought before kings and governors, and all on account of my name" (Luke 21:12).

In November 2012 an elementary school in West Marion, North Carolina ordered a little six-year-old girl to remove the word "God" from a poem she had written in honor of her two grandfathers serving in the Vietnam War.[3] Liberty Institute's 2014 Edition, Undeniable: The Survey of Hostility to Religion in America, documented Barton v. City of Balch Springs, Texas when city officials told residents of a senior center that they could not pray before their meals, listen to religious messages, or sing gospel songs because religion is banned in public buildings.[4] After the elders filed a lawsuit, government officials told them that if they had won their lawsuit their meals would be taken away because praying over government-funded meals violates separation of church and state.

In 2005 the display of the ten commandments, the visible reminder that God has standards based on caring about others, was ordered removed from three Kentucky courthouses after the ACLU filed suit in McCreary County v. ACLU, 545 U.S. 844. Both the Sixth Circuit of Appeals and the US Supreme Court ruled that the display of ten commandments is unconstitutional.

Hearing the words is how we learn of salvation. It's how the disciples learned that Jesus had risen. We are instructed, "If your brother or sister sins, go and point out their fault, just between the two of you. If they listen to you, you have won them over" (Matt 18:15) because words bring change.

---

3. Fox News, "School Orders Child to Remove God From Poem"

4. Liberty Institute, "Undeniable Survey of Religious Hostility in America 2014"

Antarctica

Words bring the compassion of the Holy Spirit, the gentle reassurance that brings joy, and supports hope. Words bring knowledge of our failings with God and the way back that brings about peace and forbearance. Hearing reveals what we are being saved from and we are quickened to exchange lies for God's truth. "Everything that is illuminated becomes a light" (Eph 5:13).

Christians are in jail in Pakistan charged with blasphemy for speaking Christ's words. Churches are burned in Nigeria and Egypt. Worshippers are slaughtered. In September 2014 reports in east Jerusalem told of young Muslim men wiring shut the door of the Living Bread Church and spraying gas at those inside. Hours before, a rock had been thrown through one of the windows.[5]

In Egypt that month a priest appealed to President Abdel Fattah El-Sisi on behalf of another church being threatened by extremists who had mobilized against a building expansion.[6] In Iraq Islamic State militants used explosives to demolish the ancient Green Church that belonged to the Assyrian Church of the East in Tikrit.

Nigeria's Kulp Bible College closed after an Islamic jihadi group, Boko Haram, killed forty-six Christians, including two pastors. The others fled the rage of the predator. They had forced their way onto the church grounds, sliced at a pastor, his wife, and daughter with a machete, then tied their hands and feet, leaving them in the living room as they set the house on fire. The gunmen then went to the church and began shooting, saying they must obliterate any trace of Christianity.

The first ISIS attack on US land happened at 7 pm on Sunday, May 3, 2015.[7] Two jihads wearing body armor drove across two states, from Phoenix to Dallas, to pull up at the Curtis Culwell Center. Picking up their rifles they began shooting at seventy-five people before a police officer shot them.

---

5. Morning Star News, "Attacks on Church in East Jerusalem Grow More Intense"

6. Ibrahim, "Christians and Churches Attacked in the West"

7. Graham, "ISIS in US Ready to Attack 'Any Target We Desire'"

Our Trees of Life

Fifteen minutes before the attack one of the shooters posted on social media accounts linked to radical Islam, "May Allah accept us as mujahideen" and pledged allegiance to "Amirul Mu'mineen," which means "the leader of the faithful." The Texas art exhibition featured cartoons of Muhammad and groups such as ISIS and the Levant. Islam prohibits depictions of its prophet. After the shooting an ISIS propagandist tweeted." Allahu Akbar!!!! 2 of our brothers just opened fire." In a radio broadcast ISIS warned, "We say to the defenders of the cross, the US, that future attacks are going to be harsher and worse. The Islamic State soldiers will inflict harm on you with the grace of God. The future is just around the corner."

The FBI reports the presence of ISIS in all fifty states of America.[8] A growing population of 100,000 Somalia Muslims live in Minneapolis and St. Paul, the country's largest pipeline to Iraq and Syria.

In Khartoum, Sudan security agents padlocked the 500-member Sudan Pentecostal Church building that has been there for twenty years, leaving its members with no place to worship.[9] Security forces reportedly raided the home of Pastor Stanislav Kim in Uzbekistan, Central Asia, detaining eleven teenagers and three adults. A new testament, a bible, and several Christian books and hymns along with computer equipment were confiscated. Voice of the Martyrs reported congregations asking, "Please pray that this pastor and his son will not face fines, but will soon be acquitted of any perceived wrongdoing. Ask God to strengthen each believer who was present during this unwarranted raid so that they will not give in to governmental intimidation and pressure, but instead be emboldened to serve our Lord faithfully."

"Please pray for us" are the words most often heard.

Isolated from the soliloquy of messages, under attack we become like trees separated from each other, unable to be alerted by companions. The fragrance of life giving words freezes into dark solid ice, helplessly stranding us in the tears of Habakkuk's voice crying to God (1:3–4):

---

8. Mora, "FBI Director: ISIS Tentacles Reach Into All 50 US States"
9. Morning Star News, "Sudan Shutters 500-Member Church in Khartoum"

> Why do you make me look at injustice? Why do you tolerate wrongdoing? Destruction and violence are before me; there is strife, and conflict abounds. Therefore the law is paralyzed, and justice never prevails. The wicked hem in the righteous, so that justice is perverted.

The Lord's response to Habakkuk did not relieve the situation, but told Habakkuk that the days ahead will be even worse because he is sending "a cruel and violent people. They will march across the world and conquer other lands. They are notorious for their cruelty and do whatever they like." Advancing like a desert wind, "they are deeply guilty for their own strength is their god."

Habakkuk cries again for God in verses 12 and 13, "Your eyes are too pure to look on evil; you cannot tolerate wrong doing. Why then do you tolerate the treacherous? Why are you silent while the wicked swallow up those more righteous than themselves?"

As 2014 entered December's Christmas, CBN in Jerusalem carried Anglican priest Andrew White's words to the world, "They chopped children in half. They chopped all heads off. How do you respond to that? That is what we have been going through. That is what we are going through." The Islamic State had demanded the Iraqi Christian children convert to Islam and say they will follow Muhammad. All under fifteen years old, before they were executed four said, "No, we love Jesus. We have always loved Jesus. We have always followed Jesus. Jesus has always been with us."[10]

In Somalia, eight Islamic gunmen infiltrated an African Union base in Mogadishu and killed fourteen peacekeepers during that year's Christmas celebrations. In Iraq the 2014 Christmas saw churches turned into prisons by the IS. Three of the Christian prisoners became ill and died without treatment. A witness, Abu Aasi, said that Christian prisoners in the churches are being forced to convert and that IS members have been breaking all the crosses. Other reports told of Christian prisoners being blindfolded, handcuffed, and held at the ancient Chaldean Church of the Immaculate Conception in eastern Mosul.[11]

10. Ibrahim, "Christmas Slaughter: Muslim Persecution of Christians"
11. Prophecy Update, "What's At Stake in Iran, Winter of Slaughter"

Elisabeth Bibi, a twenty-eight year old five-month pregnant Christian mother of four, was "beaten, scorned and humiliated, deprived of her dignity and forced to walk naked through the town" by two Muslim brothers in Pakistan. She lost her unborn baby.

"Are we only fish to be caught and killed," Habakkuk cried out. God assured Habakkuk that they will not get away with it forever. He gives Habakkuk a prophecy to write down.

For the revelation awaits an appointed time; it speaks of the end and will not prove false. Though it linger, wait for it; it will certainly come and will not delay (Hab 2:3).

God tells Habakkuk they who have plundered many nations, filled towns with violence, cut down the forests of Lebanon and destroyed the wild animals will in turn drink from the cup of the Lord's judgment.

With new insight into God's plan Habakkuk's prayer transforms. He sings:

> Pestilence marches before him; plague follows close behind. When he stops, the earth shakes. When he looks, the nations tremble. He shatters the everlasting mountains and levels the eternal hills. He is the Eternal One!

Habakkuk is given to understand that even in the most terrifying of moments God is at work for us. "Was it in anger, LORD, that you struck the rivers and parted the sea? Were you displeased with them? No, you were sending your chariots of salvation!" (v8). Reminded of the sovereign love in God's purposes, he writes down his glimpse of future days in verses 10 and 11:

> The mountains watched and trembled. Onward swept the raging waters. The mighty deep cried out, lifting its hands in submission. The sun and moon stood still in the sky as your brilliant arrows fled and your glittering spear flashed.

At the end of his book, Habakkuk pledges to trust God no matter what circumstances come upon his people.

> Yet I will wait patiently for the day of calamity to come on the nation invading us. Though the fig tree does not bud

and there are no grapes on the vines, though the olive crop fails and the fields produce no food, though there are no sheep in the pen and no cattle in the stalls, yet I will rejoice in the Lord, I will be joyful in God my Savior.

Therefore, with minds that are alert and fully sober, set your hope on the grace to be brought to you when Jesus Christ is revealed at his coming (1 Pet 1:13).

The end of all things is near. Therefore be alert and of sober mind so that you may pray (1 Pet 4:7).

This calls for patient endurance on the part of the people of God who keep his commands and remain faithful to Jesus (Rev 14:12).

A stark world such as never before experienced is ceasing the flow of Christ's healing words, leaving a landscape strewn with persecution.

Wail, you juniper, for the cedar has fallen; the stately trees are ruined!

Wail, oaks of Bashan; the dense forest has been cut down! (Zech 11:2)

> All this I have told you so that you will not fall away, Jesus told his disciples. They will put you out of the synagogue; in fact, the time is coming when anyone who kills you will think they are offering a service to God. They will do such things because they have not known the Father or me. I have told you this, so that when their time comes you will remember that I warned you about them (John 16:1–4).

Antarctica has no trees. No bushes grow here. We are left vulnerable without the protective forest that once surrounded us. A deer without shelter, pursued by predators we "thirst, as the deer pants for streams of water, so my soul pants for you, my God" (Ps 42:1). Persecution is becoming relentless, pushing against believers day and night. "My bones suffer mortal agony as my foes taunt me, saying to me all day long, Where is your God?" (v10). The psalmist says, God my Rock, "Why have you forgotten me?" (v9).

Our Trees of Life

It is the same question Jesus faced as he went to the cross. We can expect this moment.

The psalmist has lost his place of worship. "When can I go and meet with God?" (v2). He remembers "how I used to go to the house of God under the protection of the Mighty One with shouts of joy and praise among the festive throng" (v4). He remembers God "from the Land of the Jordan, the heights of Hermon—from Mount Mizar (v6). The memories of all that God has done before strengthen him.

Beneath the layers of the white continent there is evidence of trees once here, the straight ash, the sweet scent of pine, the yew and acacia that remind of the need for continuous renewal in a finite life.

Forests once grew here. There were days it was warmer, greener, hosting both warm rainforest ferns, palm trees, and baobab trees whose trunks swell to store water, and later cool mountain beech trees and conifers grew here. In 2012 researchers from the Senckenberg Research Institute and Natural History Museum took a ship to Wilkes Land off Antarctica's east coast and drilled into the Southern Ocean floor to extract sediment that contained tiny fossils of time past.[12]

From the fossilized wood and leaf impressions science estimates it was millions of years ago when forests carpeted the Antarctic, although still bathed in darkness half the year and light all during the other half. The cells in the tree's early wood show how the trees grew upward and outward. The thicker late wood grew as the trees prepared to go dormant for the winter and began storing carbon. In the mats of leaf impressions once shed in the fall and growing anew in the spring, there is an imprint of deciduous and evergreen that had stood on the now cold land. Cedars and firs, pines and oaks once lifted their arms and displayed green leaves here, leaving their footprint to echo springs of memory that God has marked by those who spoke of his promises at each tree found in the heat of the day or the buffeting storm.

---

12. Science News, "Tropical climate in the Antarctic"

The angel of the LORD came and sat down under the oak in Ophrah that belonged to Joash the Abiezrite, where his son Gideon was threshing wheat in a winepress to keep it from the Midianites (Judg 6:11).

Then you will go on from there until you reach the great tree of Tabor. Three men going up to worship God at Bethel will meet you there (1Sam 10:3).

He found him sitting under an oak tree and asked, "Are you the man of God who came from Judah?" "I am," he replied (1Kgs 13:14).

God uses his trees to show his involvement with his people across all earth's continents. "The trees of the LORD are well watered, the cedars of Lebanon that he planted. There the birds make their nests; the stork has its home in the junipers" (Ps 104:16–17). A mustering of storks fly up the country of Israel in the spring seeking rest around the Dead Sea on their way from eastern Africa. Their broad wings beat steadily, necks stretched forward and long legs extended beyond the end of their short tails. They fly to the junipers, the fir trees, the cedars on the mountains of Lebanon knowing this will keep their young safe as they build a nest from the tree's twigs. God created the tree so it would reach up sixty feet in height to spread its evergreen boughs, inviting the birds to find rest among its branches.

Come to me, all you who are weary and burdened, and I will give you rest, Jesus said (Matt 11:28).

After Jesus was done speaking with his disciples, he prayed, "Father, the hour has come" (John 17:1, 14–18). "I have given them your word and the world has hated them, for they are not of the world any more than I am of the world. My prayer is not that you take them out of the world but that you protect them from the evil one."

He said, "My prayer is not for them alone. I pray also for those who will believe in me through their message. Righteous Father, though the world does not know you, I know you, and they know that you have sent me. I have made you known to them, and will continue to make you known in order that the love you have for me may be in them and that I myself may be in them." God's word cannot be stopped. "It will not return to me empty, but will accomplish what I desire and achieve the purpose for which I sent it" (Isa 55:11).

As we speak words of the way of Jesus, we bring streams of water into a drought. We bring God's love for Jesus. In neighborhoods increasingly untrustworthy God plants the trees, the people who hold up the standard of his words, sensitive to the changing climate around us. They are a force of nature, bringing communion with the Lord through quiet prayer, through speech and song that are leaves of words absorbing light and bringing food to our growth.

Threats of violence and the heavy hand of the courtrooms can produce the fruit of desolation, anger, letting go of God's instructions for life. Because we will not be taken out of the battle, we are to stand in its midst and glorify God. We know the battle will end. "He makes wars cease to the ends of the earth" (Ps 46:9). David guarded his heart from despair by continually giving thanks through his battles. "My heart, O God, is steadfast; I will sing and make music with all my soul" (Ps 108:1). The Hebrew word for steadfast, *kuwn*, means to be established, rooted, used to describe a house on a stable foundation and a person enduring in the way David's joy in the Lord was unconquerable in his music, helped by the gift of the trees.

The jubilance is evergreen in the cypress lending itself to make harps and timbrels played by the people to sing thanks when they carried the ark of the covenant of the Lord (2Sam 6:5). In a world that is casting gloom with immeasurable coldness, God's trees uphold the rafters over the covenant between Christ and his believers. "The beams of our house are cedars; our rafters are fir" (Song 17). We are told to keep growing leaves and singing his song. Keep reaching toward heaven, keep rooted because Christ will return.

Isaiah shares with us what our world will be like then. "For you shall go out with joy, and be led forth with peace; the mountains and the hills shall break forth before you into singing, and all the trees of the field shall clap their hands (Isa 55:12). In verse 13 Isaiah wanted us to know, "Instead of the thorn shall come up the fir tree, and instead of the brier shall come up the myrtle tree: and it shall be to the LORD for a name, for an everlasting sign that shall not be cut off." The trees shall not be afflicted ever again. The thorns of life will not prick us. The protections of the hawthorn will not be needed because the Lord himself will border us.

This communion is symbolized in the tree in the fourteen chapters of the book of Hosea. His heart was broken with pain too great to bear because Israel's faithlessness tore the nation away from relationship with God. Hosea spoke to his nation telling the people that they could come home to God's outstretched arms. He says, "Take words with you and return to the Lord. Say to him: Forgive all our sins and receive us graciously, that we may offer the fruit of our lips." The Lord said to tell them:

> I will be like the dew to Israel, he will blossom like a lily. Like a cedar of Lebanon he will send down his roots; his young shoots will grow. His splendor will be like an olive tree, his fragrance like a cedar of Lebanon. People will dwell again in his shade; they will flourish like the grain, they will blossom like the vine (Hos 14:5–7).

I am like a flourishing juniper, Hosea decides (v8). His joy with the Lord would not be taken. The winds shivering the trees, the storms kick up dust to blind us from seeing and we don't always feel the refreshing strength of the pines and cedars. Aching with thirst we send our roots deeper and God provides. "Without me you can do nothing," Jesus told us, in compassion for our struggle (John 15:5).

Antarctica is too cold to be there for very long. Scientists come and study the ice, camping in tents or working on the decks of research ships in the Southern Ocean, supplied with nutrition, heavy clothing, and technology. Tourists visit in summer when the day is long and the raft of female penguins make their way home about the time their eggs hatch. It's a place where meteorites falling through the tempest sky are easily found in the white ice.

It's a place teaching us what our world could be like without the shelter of the trees. Even in the storms whipping the earth and pivoting lightning through the galaxies, "that hour which is about to come upon the whole world, to test those who dwell on the earth" will bring God's Son who will "make them know that I have loved you" (Rev 3:9–10).

The Antarctic is dropping pebbles from the ice shelves, strewn on the bottom of the ocean where undiscovered fish live in an underwater world. Scientists from the University of Nebraska-Lincoln were the first to view this untouched world in January 2015 when they drilled through 2,400 feet of ice to view the hidden depths.[13] They say it signals a collapse of the ice shelf that would set glaciers flowing more quickly into the ocean, raising global sea levels that swallow islands and spread over land.

This is one of man's last discoveries, reminding of the mystery beyond the frozen expanse of dark glass separating mankind from God's throne in heaven, thinning too as the sacrifice of Jesus makes a way for us to return to God and Jesus return to us.

Prayer is our plea for his presence.

"Blessed are those who have not seen and yet have believed," Jesus said (John 20:29). He told us to remember, "I am the vine; you are the branches. If you remain in me and I in you, you will bear much fruit." That person who is like a tree planted by streams of water is that "whose delight is in the law of the Lord, and who meditates on his law day and night." His leaf will not wither but continue to seek light to strengthen the tree.

For the Spirit God gave us does not make us timid, but gives us power, love and self-discipline (2Tim 1:7).

The fruit of the Spirit brings this self control (Gal 5:23). Against such choice there is no law, not even the vast Antarctic tundra that brings us no provision, no shelter, no comfort. Even this belongs to our God. Even the forgiveness of our enemies belongs to him.

A man without self-control is like a city broken into and left without walls (Prov 25:28). In Ezekiel's time false prophets made

---

13. Fox, "Discovery: Fish Live beneath Antarctic"

no distinction between the holy and the profane. The people of the land were accused of practicing oppression without justice and presenting the unclean as clean. God told Ezekiel, "I looked for someone among them who would build up the wall and stand before me in the gap on behalf of the land" (Eze 22:30).

In difficult days the eyes of the Lord look across the earth so he can give his strong support to those whose hearts call to him (2Chr 16:9). He is there with those who, like Ezra, stand in the gate for their generation, reading out the words of God to say here is the way to enter, here are the words summoning them from death. Peter indicated that growth will "make every effort to add to your faith goodness; and to goodness, knowledge; and to knowledge, self-control; and to self-control, perseverance; and to perseverance, godliness; and to godliness, mutual affection; and to mutual affection, love. For if you possess these qualities in increasing measure, they will keep you from being ineffective and unproductive in your knowledge of our Lord Jesus Christ" (2Pet 1:5–8).

Without that interlocking unfolding growth, judgment is shown to us through the loss of trees. "He brings princes to naught and reduces the rulers of this world to nothing. No sooner are they planted, no sooner are they sown, no sooner do they take root in the ground, than he blows on them and they wither, and a whirlwind sweeps them away like chaff" (Isa 40:23–24).

We become shelterless.

Nebuchadnezzer told Daniel of his dream.

> The tree grew large and strong and its top touched the sky; it was visible to the ends of the earth. Its leaves were beautiful, its fruit abundant, and on it was food for all. Under it the wild animals found shelter, and the birds lived in its branches; from it every creature was fed.
>
> In the visions I saw while lying in bed, I looked, and there before me was a holy one, a messenger, coming down from heaven. He called in a loud voice: "Cut down the tree and trim off its branches; strip off its leaves and scatter its fruit. Let the animals flee from under it and the birds from its branches" (Dan 4:11–13).

Daniel tells Nebuchadnezzer that he is the tree whose kingdom has expanded across the land, but he will be cast down because he'd come to believe in his own greatness. The command to leave the stump with its roots meant that his kingdom would be restored when he acknowledges that heaven rules (v26). Daniel counsels with him to renounce his own ways and give the glory to God.

Through Christ's perspective as he struggled in the garden Gethsemane, the pruning that causes temporary pain is extending the roots seeking the eternal gift. From the cross he looked out upon us, his eyes scanned the horizon and saw us. He thirsted with a love aching for us to return to God. He thirsted for our enemies to be reconciled. He prepared his disciples to submit to what he's promised, as the trees, the ocean waves, the quaking earth submit in trust to his plan. The fruit becomes evident. Paul spoke of its influence in his letter, "When we are cursed, we bless; when we are persecuted, we endure it; when we are slandered, we answer kindly. We have become the scum of the earth, the garbage of the world—right up to this moment" (1Cor 4:12–13).

Against this fruit there is no accusation, "For through the law I died to the law so that I might live for God" (Gal 2:19).

Christ's people are compared to a green olive tree in the house of God (Ps 52:8). A Christian is compared to a tree planted by the rivers to bring about fruit in season (Ps 1:3) Those rooted in God's living waters are compared to palm trees of victory and the cedar tree that offers shade to those in need of compassion (Ps 92). Our branches reach toward the light where we have only to bring a problem to the throne of mercy and ask to be "like a green fir tree" through all seasons, reminded we are adorned with garments of praise, clothed with fragrance, leafing with words of hope.

Earth hurtles through space carrying the choir of God's trees singing through the stars. The tree became a world motif understood everywhere expressing our yearning to connect to heaven, bottle up its light, be rooted in wells of quenching, have shelter, and offer provision. The Norse spoke of the ash tree supported by roots that extend to far off springs of water. The Siberians saw the tree as connecting the realities of the physical and spiritual. It's used as a symbol that joins the Three Kingdoms of Korea. Ancient Greek stories told of the tree that holds the earth being sawed at by goblins. Trees of life are found carved into furniture and decorations of the Lithuanians. There is a wish-fulfilling tree in south Asian belief systems. Persian mythology tells of a world tree that bears all seeds. When an enemy created a frog to destroy the tree so no trees could grow on earth, the legend says Creator made two fish to guard the tree. Ancient Iran mythology held that two trees were ancestors of all life. Chinese folklore tells of a tree that produces fruit to give eternal life. Trees are often planted over graves or at four corners of ceremonial sites to mark the cardinal directions. The Egyptian's sycamore stood representing the door between life and death. To the Maya, the ceiba tree represents the tree of life.

The axis mundi, the tall trunk is a stable center that connects the earth below with branches that canopy in the sky above as we spin in an ever-changing cosmo of births and loss.

In Jewish and Christian teachings a tree sits at the center of both heaven and earth's gardens. At creation the original sin of the tree in the first garden corrupted the world. The fruit of the tree of life is our eucharist, the body of Christ that was nailed to the tree. Referring to the Torah as a tree of life we've inherited laws and stories that preserve wisdom, love for God, and compassion for his creations. "Her ways are pleasant ways, and all her paths are peace" (Prov 3:17). She is the tree of life described in the book of Revelation with healing in its leaves for all nations.

Antarctica's night is a deep infinite darkness. The only tree that remains in our midst is the tree that made the cross, the tree that translates our tears into praise. The silence of Antarctica bids us to listen. There are no other voices here. There is only the strain to hear the holy one of God. "I am convinced that nothing can ever separate us from God's love," Paul said. "Neither death nor life, neither angels nor demons, neither our fears for today nor our worries about tomorrow—not even the powers of hell can separate us from God's love" (Rom 8:38).

At the foot of this tree, there are thousands gathered, millions from across the generations. It is the doorway through which we pass the flaming sword at the edge of Eden that block us from the tree of life. Jesus promised, "Blessed are those who wash their robes, that they may have the right to the tree of life and may go through the gates into the city" (Rev 22:14). We enter by hearing the words of Christ. No storm on earth is able to keep his believers from the shade of this cross.

"No power in the sky above or in the earth below—indeed, nothing in all creation will ever be able to separate us from the love of God that is revealed in Christ Jesus our Lord," Paul said. In prison, in chains, before courts, to his own people as well as to other cultures, Paul urged people to listen.

Stop listening to instruction, my son, and you will stray from the words of knowledge (Prov 19:27).

Turning your ear to wisdom and applying your heart to understanding (Prov 2:2).

Don't be unwilling, Paul said. Be angry, but don't sin. Be silent and hear God's promise to restore the wasteland, how he will raise people from all around the world from the seeds that begin as words spoken. Be still and see in the heartland of crushing cold there is a cross still standing.

Antarctica's frozen expanse offers less than 1 percent of its water for plants in the cracks inside rocks and sandstone around the edge of the continent. Life is found in the moss and lichens and two species of flowering plants.

The slender blades of leaves of the Antarctic hair grass emerge folded as they grow into long dark green stems. Clusters are visible along the coast welcoming the summer, its flowers forming seeds in the long growing season. Antarctic pearlwort's cup shaped yellow and white flowers shine upward to the sky, its tiny leaves reducing water loss along the western and northern peninsula where it finds the mildest cold.

These frigid desert soils are the least diverse habitats on earth. In our lives it may mean any number of sacrifices that we've given up for his kingdom —employment, relationship, possessions — or it may mean we suffer pain or physical torture because we have witnessed his words to others.

In quietness and trust is your strength (Isa 30:15).

The judgments striking the earth and parting the sea of people are making a way for the chariots of salvation that Habbakuk foresaw. Weathering these storms clarifies our doubts. Innately a part of us, even John the Baptist who boldly confronted Herod warning him of doing wrong, experienced growing doubt after being locked for months in a prison east of the Dead Sea. In prolonged isolation he began to question his own beliefs and sent two of his disciples to walk down through the Jordan Valley, find Jesus and ask, "Are you the one who is to come, or should we expect someone else?"

What caused his doubt? John who recognized Jesus from the womb, who took the vow of the Nazarene, baptized others into the hope, a voice in the wilderness, even he experienced doubt after being separated to a time when there was no more hope for his life in the world of tomorrow (Luke 7:18–23). Is this how you love us Lord?

Habakkuk in his endless night glimpsed the coming of Jesus. He wrote, "His brilliant splendor fills the heavens, and the earth is filled with his praise. His coming is as brilliant as the sunrise. Rays of light flash from his hands, where his awesome power is hidden" (Hab 3:3–4). No longer seeing himself as a deer hunted down by the enemy, Habakkuk exclaims, "The Sovereign LORD is my strength; he makes my feet like the feet of a deer, he enables me to tread on the heights" (Hab 3:19).

The morning star will return. We will see the bloom of the white lily. We will touch the tree of life green with healing leaves.

Trees bearing this hope are rooted, determined in their thirst for his waters. Each branch has grown from the root of Christ, each grafted in from around all the earth, reaching skyward turned toward the sun to share the promise Jesus sent after he ascended. "I, Jesus, have sent my angel to give you this testimony for the churches. I am the Root and the Offspring of David, and the bright Morning Star" (Rev 22:16).

We are pulled by the Morning Star into orbit around him.

When God took Abraham outside, he told him, "Look up at the sky and count the stars—if indeed you can count them." Then he said to him, "So shall your offspring be" (Gen 15:5). We, on this side of the stars, view the stellar twinkling through layers of turbulent air encompassing the earth. The dots of light, like the children of Abraham's faith, help us navigate through the darkening night, remaining luminary as we are held around the sun that gives us life.

The LORD will fight for you; you need only to be still (Exod 14:14).

BIBLIOGRAPHY

The ABC, "Giant kelp forests granted endangered status," August 19, 2012 Web. http://www.abc.net.au/news/2012-08-19/giant-kelp-forests-listed-as-endangered/4208174

Alexander, Ruth, "Are there really 100,000 new Christian martyrs every year." BBC News, November 12, 2013. Web. http://www.bbc.com/news/magazine-24864587

Alford, Deann and Morgan, Timothy C. "Terrorism Charge Snares Prominent American Missionary." Christianity Today, March 23, 2015 Web. www.christianitytoday.com/.../terrorism-american-missionaries

Associated Press."1,000 join Muslim ring of peace outside Oslo synagogue," February 22, 2015, Web. http://www.usatoday.com/story/news/world/2015/02/22/ring-of-peace/23834625/

Australia Bureau of Statistics, "Australian Social Trends," November 20, 2013. Web. http://www.abs.gov.au/ausstats/abs@.nsf/Lookup/4102.0Main+Features30Nov+2013

Australian Census of Population and Housing. Web. http://www.abs.gov.au/ausstats/abs@.nsf/Lookup/2077.0main+features22006-2011

Baobab Superfruit, "Ethical Trade and Sustainability." Web. http://baobabsuperfruit.com/the-ethics/

Barnabas Fund, Web. https://barnabasfund.org

Barnabas Fund, "Boko Haram reveals fate of abducted schoolgirls, continues atrocities in Northern Nigeria," November 6, 2014 Web. https://barnabasfund.org/news/Boko-Haram-reveals-fate-of-abducted-schoolgirls-continues-atrocities-in-Northern-Nigeria

Barnabas Fund, "Lao Hmong Christian families evicted after converting to Christianity, "November 19, 2011 Web. https://barnabasfund.org/news/Lao-Hmong-Christian-families-evicted-after-converting-to-Christianity

BBC News, "Gay cake row," November 6, 2014. Web. http://www.bbc.com/news/uk-northern-ireland-29926372

BBC News. "Young Australian women trying to join IS," May 29, 2015 Web. http://www.bbc.com/news/world-australia-32926114

Bibliography

Boland, Barbara, "Christians Killed in Nigeria Through June Already at 91 percent of 2013's Full-Year Total." CNS News, June 29, 2014 Web http://cnsnews.com/mrctv-blog/barbara-boland/christians-killed-nigeria-through-june-already-91-2013-s-full-year-total

Botelho, Greg, "Kenya's Garissa University College awakens to Islamic militant terror," April 3, 2015. CNN News. Web. http://www.cnn.com/2015/04/02/africa/kenya-university-attack-scene/

Campaign to Stop GE Trees. Web. http://stopgetrees.org/category/pressroom/

CBS News. "Hospital Bans Christmas Carolers From Singing Religious Songs," December 24, 2013 Web. http://atlanta.cbslocal.com/2013/12/24/hospital-bans-christmas-carolers-from-singing-religious-songs/

The Central Bureau of Statistics (Israel) Web. http://www1.cbs.gov.il/reader/cw_usr_view_Folder?ID=141

Church in Chains, "India: Pastor and carol singers attacked by Hindu extremists," December 23, 2014 Web. http://www.churchinchains.ie/node/763

Climate Emergency Institute. "2 Degrees Celsius." Web. http://www.climateemergencyinstitute.com/2c.html

Cook, Bill. "Some Exotic Species Are Useful and Benign." The St. Ignace News. December 11, 2014 Web. http://www.stignacenews.com/news/2014-12-11/News/Some_Exotic_Species_Are_Useful_and_Benign_But_Many.html

Culture News, "Supremes Rule Bible as Hate Speech in Canada," March 18, 2013 Web. http://culturecampaign.blogspot.com/2013/03/supremes-rule-bible-as-hate-speech-in.html

DeCaro, Joseph, "Deported Messianic Jew to Appeal Supreme Court." Worthy Christian News, October 12, 2014 Web. http://www.worthynews.com/18016-deported-messianic-jew-to-appeal-supreme-court

DeCaro, Joseph, "Ethiopian Officials Destroy Evangelical Church." Worthy Christian News, December 9, 2014 Web. http://www.worthynews.com/18142-ethiopian-officials-destroy-evangelical-church

DeCaro, Joseph, "Islamic Herdsmen Again Attack Christians in Benue, Nigeria." Worthy Christian News, December 30, 2014, Web. http://www.worthynews.com/18162-islamist-herdsmen-again-attack-christians-in-benue-nigeria

DeCaro, Joseph, "Pastor Jailed for Displaying Anti-Abortion Sign." Worthy Christian News, May 22, 2014. Web. http://www.worthychristianforums.com/topic/180181-pastor-jailed-for-displaying-anti-abortion-sign/

DeCaro, Joseph, "Two Christians Fined by Kazakhan courts." Worthy Christian News. Web. http://www.christianpersecution.info/two-christians-fined-by-kazakhan-courts/

Dean, Jamie, "The ISIS war against the people of the cross." World Magazine. February 17, 2015. Web. www.worldmag.com/the_isis_war_against_the_people_of_the_cross

Bibliography

Durie, Mark, "One Hundred Years of Jihad in Australia." Middle East Forum, January 1, 2015 Web. http://www.meforum.org/4947/one-hundred-years-of-jihad-in-australia

Evangel.fm, "Sudan Air Force Bombs Church Complex in Nuba Mountains," October 16, 2013 Web. http://evangel.fm/english/sudan-air-force-bombs-church-complex-nuba-mountains/

Fadel, Leila, "ISIS Beheadings in Libya Devastate an Egyptian Village." NPR, February 17, 2015 Web. http://www.npr.org/sections/parallels/2015/02/17/386986424/isis-beheadings-in-libya-devastate-an-egyptian-village

Farbishel, David, "Christian Persecution: Of Whom the World is Not Worthy." Grand Canyon University, March 25, 2015 Web. http://blogs.gcu.edu/college-of-theology/christian-persecution-of-whom-the-world-was-not-worthy/

Fox, Douglas, "Discovery: Fish Live beneath Antarctic." Scientific American. January 21, 2015 Web. http://www.scientificamerican.com/article/discovery-fish-live-beneath-antarctica/

Fox News, "CA Teacher Tells 1st-Grader to Stop Talking About the Bible," January 15, 2014 Web. http://insider.foxnews.com/2014/01/15/ca-teacher-tells-1st-grader-brynn-williams-stop-talking-about-bible

Fox News, "School Orders Child to Remove God From Poem," November 29, 2012 Web. http://radio.foxnews.com/toddstarnes/top-stories/school-orders-child-to-remove-god-from-poem.html

Golovnina, Maria, "Glimmer of hope for shrinking Aral Sea." Reuters, June 24, 2008 Web. http://www.reuters.com/article/2008/06/24/us-kazakhstan-aralsea-idUSL2262226020080624

Graham, Efrem, "ISIS in US Ready to Attack 'Any Target We Desire.'" CBN News, May 6, 2015 Web. http://www.cbn.com/cbnnews/us/2015/May/ISIS-in-US-Ready-to-Attack-Any-Target-We-Desire/

Gray, Louise, "Toxic caterpillar warning as infestation of oak moths spread." The Telegraph, May 5, 2013 Web. http://www.telegraph.co.uk/news/earth/earthnews/10038532/Toxic-caterpillar-warning-as-infestation-of-oak-moths-spreads.html

Humantrafficking.org, "Report on Trafficking in Australia," July 2005 Web. http://www.humantrafficking.org/updates/8

Ibrahim, Raymond, "Christians and Churches Attacked in the West." Gatestone Institute, December 24, 2014 Web. http://www.gatestoneinstitute.org/4966/christians-churches-attacked/

Ibrahim, Raymond, "Christmas Slaughter: Muslim Persecution of Christians." Gatestone Institute, February 1, 2015 Web. http://www.gatestoneinstitute.org/5169/christmas-slaughter-muslim-persecution

International Union for Conservation of Nature, "The IUCN Red List of Threatened Species." Web. http://www.iucnredlist.org/

Jewish National Fund: Plant Trees in Israel, Web. http://www.jnf.org/work-we-do/our-projects/forestry-ecology/

Bibliography

Jewish Reconstructionist Community, Trees of the Bible, Web. www.jewishrecon.org/resource/trees-bible

Johnson, Todd, "Religious Freedom Project." Berkeley Center for Religion, Peace & World Affairs, Georgetown University, August 25, 2014, Web. http://berkleycenter.georgetown.edu/responses/the-shifting-patterns-of-global-christian-persecution

The Kabbalah Center, "What is Kabbalah" Web. http://kabbalah.com

Kimani, Mary, "Taking on violence against women in Africa." Africa Renewal, July 2007 Web. http://www.un.org/africarenewal/magazine/july-2007/taking-violence-against-women-africa

Liberty Institute, "Undeniable Survey of Religious Hostility in America 2014," Web. https://www.libertyinstitute.org/pages/survey-of-religious-hostilities

Marshall, Paul, "The War on Christians." Hudson Institute, June 23, 2014 Web. http://www.hudson.org/research/10364-the-war-on-christians

McGraw, Daniel, "Is Christianity in America losing ground?" Christian Chronicle, May 13, 2009 Web. http://www.christianchronicle.org/article/is-christianity-in-america-losing-ground

Mora, Edwin, "FBI Director: ISIS Tentacles Reach Into All 50 US States." Breitbart News, February 26, 2015 Web. http://www.breitbart.com/big-government/2015/02/26/fbi-director-isis-tentacles-reach-into-all-50 u-s-states/

Morning Star News, "Attacks on Church in East Jerusalem Grow More Intense," September 30, 2014 Web. http://morningstarnews.org/2014/09/attacks-on-church-in-east-jerusalem-grow-more-intense/

Morning Star News, "Columbian Guerrilla Group Bans Worship Services and Threatens Pastors," December 18, 2013 Web. http://morningstarnews.org/2013/12/colombian-guerrilla-group-bans-worship-services-threatens-pastors/

Morning Star News, "Muslim Extremists Kill 31 Christians in Taraba State, Nigeria." October 24, 2014 Web. http://morningstarnews.org/2014/10/muslim-extremists-kill-31-christians-in-taraba-state-nigeria/

Morning Star News, "Police in Sudan attack worshipping congregation, arrest 38 Congregants," December 5, 2014 Web. http://www.layman.org/police-sudan-attack-worshiping-congregation-arrest-38-christians/

Morning Star News, "Sudan Shutters 500-Member Church in Khartoum," September 3, 2014 Web. http://morningstarnews.org/2014/09/sudan-shutters-500-member-church-in-khartoum/

National Center for Historic Memory, Web, http://www.centrodememoriahistorica.gov.co/informes/informes-2013/item/165-guerrilla-y-poblacion-civil-trayectoria-de-las-farc-1949–2013

The Nature Conservancy, "Rainforest Facts" Web. http://www.nature.org/ourinitiatives/urgentissues/rainforests/rainforests-facts.xml

Organization of American States, "Report: Indigenous Peoples Voluntary Isolation," December 30, 2013 Web. http://www.oas.org/en/iachr/

BIBLIOGRAPHY

indigenous/docs/pdf/Report-Indigenous-Peoples-Voluntary-Isolation.pdf

Pew Forum, "America's Changing Religious Landscape," December 5, 2015 Web. www.pewforum.org/2015/05/12/americas-changing-religious-landscape

Pew Forum, "Global Christianity, The Size and Distribution of the World's Christian Population." December 19, 2011 Web. http://www.pewforum.org/2011/12/19/global-christianity

Pray for Pastor Saeed Abedini Web. https://www.facebook.com/PrayForPastorSaeedAbedini

Prophecy Update, "What's At Stake in Iran, Winter of Slaughter," February 3, 2015 Web. http://prophecyupdate.blogspot.com/2015/02/whats-at-stake-with-iran-winter-of.html

Science News, "Tropical climate in the Antarctic," August 1, 2012 Web, http://www.sciencedaily.com/releases/2012/08/120801132339.htm

Scientific News Service, "Trees Send Distress Signals to Birds When Attacked by Insects," October 10, 2013 Web. http://www.agenciasinc.es/en/News/Trees-send-distress-signals-to-birds-when-attacked-by-insects

Sedlock, Mike "Mish," "VA Refuses Christmas Cards from 51 School Kids Intended for Disabled Veterans." Freedom Outpost, December 26, 2013 Web. http://freedomoutpost.com/2013/12/va-refuses-christmas-cards-51-school-kids-intended-disabled-veterans/

Smith, Samuel, "Nigerian Pastor Butchered to Death." Christian Post, January 30, 2015 Web. http://www.christianpost.com/news/nigerian-pastor-butchered-to-death-by-muslim-herdsmen-remembered-as-dedicated-servant-to-the-poor-who-educated-over-400-kids-for-free-133371/

Space.com, "Meteor Blast Over Russia," Feb. 15, February 27, 2013 Web. http://www.space.com/19823-russia-meteor-explosion-complete-coverage.html

Stahl, Julie and Mitchell, Chris, "Christians, Jews Team Up to Fight Against Islamic Persecution." CBN News, October 19, 2014 Web. http://www.cbn.com/cbnnews/insideisrael/2014/October/Christians-Jews-Team-Up-to-Fight-Islamic-Persecution/

Starnes, Todd, "What's-going-on-at-Air-Force-Academy-God's-Word-vs-Pentagon's-Word." Fox News, March 13, 2014 Web. http://www.foxnews.com/opinion/2014/03/13/what-going-on-at-air-force-academy-god-word-vs-pentagon-word.html

United Nations Forum on Forests, Tenth Session, April 8 to 19, 2013 Web. http://www.un.org/esa/forests/pdf/session_documents/unff10/EcoContrForests.pdf

United Nations Office of Drugs and Crime, "World Drug Report 2014." Web. https://www.unodc.org/documents/wdr2014/World_Drug_Report_2014_web.pdf

US Commission on International Religious Freedom, Russia, Web. http://www.uscirf.gov/sites/default/files/Russia%202015.pdf

BIBLIOGRAPHY

US Department of State, Columbia, "International Religious Freedom Report 2004." Web. http://www.state.gov/j/drl/rls/irf/2004/35531.htm

Vazquez, Maegan, "Arizona Man Sent to Jail for Holding Bible Studies in His Home." Fox News, August 5, 2012 Web. http://www.foxnews.com/us/2012/08/05/arizona-man-sent-to-jail-for-holding-bible-studies-in-his-home/

Voice of the Persecuted, "Christians Killed." Web. https://voiceofthepersecuted.wordpress.com/tag/christians-killed/

Werren, Garry, "Environmental Weeds of the Wet Tropics." John Carroll University, January 2001 Web. https://research.jcu.edu.au/tropwater/resources/01%2004%20WeedsReport.pdf

World Watch List, Open Doors Web. www.opendoorsuk.org/persecution/country_profiles.php

Worthy Christian News, "Hospital Employee Ordered to Remove God Bless America From Email Signature," May 15, 2014 Web. http://www.worthynews.com/13105-hospital-employee-ordered-to-remove-god-bless-america-from-email-signature

Worthy Christian News, "Pakistan: Christian Couple Burned Alive," November 9, 2014 Web. http://www.worthynews.com/18079-pakistan-christian-couple-burned-alive

www.ingramcontent.com/pod-product-compliance
Lightning Source LLC
Chambersburg PA
CBHW071438160426
43195CB00013B/1953